$21.95

W9-CLL-341

Understanding

I Am the Cheese

New and future titles in the Understanding Great Literature series include:

Understanding *The Catcher in the Rye*
Understanding *Flowers for Algernon*
Understanding *Hamlet*
Understanding *The Outsiders*
Understanding *Romeo and Juliet*
Understanding *The Yearling*

Understanding

I Am
the Cheese

UNDERSTANDING GREAT LITERATURE

Jennifer Keeley

Lucent Books
P.O. Box 289011
San Diego, CA 92198-9011

On cover: Robert Cormier, author of *I Am the Cheese.*

Library of Congress Cataloging-in-Publication Data

Keeley, Jennifer, 1974–
    Understanding I am the cheese / by Jennifer Keeley.
    p. cm. — (Understanding great literature)
    Includes bibliographical references and index.
    Summary: An introduction to Robert Cormier's book, "I am the
    Cheese," discussing the author's life, the impact of the book,
    plot, cast of characters, and literary criticism.
    ISBN 1-56006-678-4 (alk. paper)
    1. Cormier, Robert. I am the cheese—Juvenile literature.
[1. Cormier, Robert. I am the cheese. 2 American literature—
History and criticism.] I. Title. II. Series.
    PS3553.O653 K44 2001
    813'.54—dc21
                                                        00-008170

Contents

FOREWORD

"Except for a living man, there is nothing more wonderful than a book!" wrote the widely respected nineteenth-century teacher and writer Charles Kingsley. A book, he continued, "is a message to us from human souls we never saw. And yet these [books] arouse us, terrify us, teach us, comfort us, open our hearts to us as brothers." There are many different kinds of books, of course; and Kingsley was referring mainly to those containing literature—novels, plays, short stories, poems, and so on. In particular, he had in mind those works of literature that were and remain widely popular with readers of all ages and from many walks of life.

Such popularity might be based on one or several factors. On the one hand, a book might be read and studied by people in generation after generation because it is a literary classic, with characters and themes of universal relevance and appeal. Homer's epic poems, the *Iliad* and the *Odyssey*, Chaucer's *Canterbury Tales*, Shakespeare's *Hamlet* and *Romeo and Juliet*, and Dickens's *A Christmas Carol* fall into this category. Some popular books, on the other hand, are more controversial. Mark Twain's *Huckleberry Finn* and J.D. Salinger's *The Catcher in the Rye*, for instance, have their legions of devoted fans who see them as great literature; while others view them as less than worthy because of their racial depictions, profanity, or other factors.

Still another category of popular literature includes realistic modern fiction, including novels such as Robert Cormier's *I Am the Cheese* and S.E. Hinton's *The Outsiders*. Their keen social insights and sharp character portrayals have consistently reached out to and captured the imaginations of many teenagers and young adults; and for this reason they are often assigned and studied in schools.

These and other similar works have become the "old standards" of the literary scene. They are the ones that people most often read, discuss, and study; and each has, by virtue of its content, critical success, or just plain longevity, earned the right to be the subject of a book examining its content. (Some, of course, like the *Iliad* and *Hamlet*, have been the subjects of numerous books already; but their literary stature is so lofty that there can never be too many books about them!) For millions of readers and students in one generation after another, each of these works becomes, in a sense, an adventure in appreciation, enjoyment, and learning.

The main purpose of Lucent's Understanding Great Literature series is to aid the reader in that ongoing literary adventure. Each volume in the series focuses on a single literary work that a majority of critics and teachers view as a classic and/or that is widely studied and discussed in schools. A typical volume first tells why the work in question is important. Then follow detailed overviews of the author's life, the work's historical background, its plot, its characters, and its themes. Numerous quotes from the work, as well as by critics and other experts, are interspersed throughout and carefully documented with footnotes for those who wish to pursue further research. Also included is a list of ideas for essays and other student projects relating to the work, an appendix of literary criticisms and analyses by noted scholars, and a comprehensive annotated bibliography.

The great nineteenth-century American poet Henry David Thoreau once quipped: "Read the best books first, or you may not have a chance to read them at all." For those who are reading or about to read the "best books" in the literary canon, the comprehensive, thorough, and thoughtful volumes of the Understanding Great Literature series are indispensable guides and sources of enrichment.

Challenging Assumptions

In the publishing industry, books that appeal to readers between the approximate ages of twelve and twenty are classified as young adult fiction. This category of fiction faces a unique problem—many of its authors are adults and, therefore, not part of the teen audience for which their novels are written. In order to write, these adult authors must ponder what subjects they believe young people want to read about and consider the reading level of the teen audience. Then, they write books they believe young people will both want to read and be capable of reading. However, these decisions are based on assumptions about what issues writers and publishers feel young readers can understand. Of course, inherent in such assumptions is a belief that some subjects—or even writing styles—are either too mature or too sophisticated for a younger audience. Robert Cormier's novel *I Am the Cheese* discounted some of these beliefs and asked publishers, writers, and critics of young adult fiction to question some of their everyday assumptions about teen readers.

When *I Am the Cheese* was published in 1977 it was an oddity in young adult fiction. The majority of teen novels were about personal discovery and ended happily. Girls came to decisions about who to take to the prom; boys successfully stood up to bullies; and bad guys got what was coming to them.

Even if a book was about a more serious issue such as drug use, characters found solutions which left them happy or at least hopeful. Stories such as these were told in a straightforward way as readers followed a protagonist through a day, a week, or a year. It was standard practice to write young adult books about personal discovery that ended happily and were easy for teens to read.

Amid books about personal discovery, *I Am the Cheese* dealt with political matters such as organized crime and government corruption. The novel ended unhappily with the protagonist facing certain death. Yet this type of break with the conventions of young adult literature was to be expected from Cormier. After all, his first young adult novel, *The Chocolate War*, published three years earlier, had also broken these taboos.

Although the fact that Cormier refused to sugarcoat the world for young readers may have come as no surprise the second time around, *I Am the Cheese* broke with another accepted practice of young adult fiction. The structure and style of the book were incredibly complex. So much so that one irate reviewer was compelled to exclaim that it was "no laughing matter," and to wonder "why novels should be specially written for such readers at all"[1] if authors were to confound the conventions and create such complex narratives.

These remarks are an excellent illustration of the impact of *I Am the Cheese*. Behind the anger is an assumption that novels "specially written" for teen readers should not have complex narratives. Yet young readers were eagerly consuming Cormier's novel.

Similarly, books about personal discovery with happy endings dominated young adult fiction because another assumption was routinely made about teen readers. Specifically, as Patricia Head suggests, young adult fiction "could, or should, comfort its readers."[2] A happy or hopeful ending is comforting and came to be one of the conventions of young adult literature. Cormier's work ignored the standard and the young audience assented.

Thus, *I Am the Cheese* was an anomaly in young adult fiction because it expected a great deal more of its adolescent reader, a fact for which Cormier originally apologized to his editor. However, he soon learned—as did many people working in the field of young adult fiction—that more could be expected. In fact, young people seemed to be pleased and excited to pick up this challenging book. As a result, *I Am the Cheese* was commercially successful and solidified Robert Cormier's place in young adult fiction. The success of the book, in turn, forced authors, publishers, and other adults both to reevaluate the capabilities of young readers and to reconsider what the teen audience wanted to read. In this way, *I Am the Cheese* helped change old assumptions about adolescent readers and opened the field of young adult fiction to a broader and more challenging range of styles and subject matter.

CHAPTER ONE

The Life of Robert Cormier

The story of Robert Cormier's life, both past and present, takes place in the small New England town of Leominster, Massachusetts. Robert C. Laserte, the president of the city's historical society, describes present-day Leominster as "a beautiful City nestled in a natural valley surrounded by rambling hills. . . . The air is excellent, being 400 feet above sea level. . . . Leominster combines the advantages of both city and country life without the disadvantages of high cost and high frenzy."[3]

The town is located about forty miles west of the bustling metropolis of Boston, Massachusetts, and boasts a population of more than thirty-five thousand citizens. However, most readers of Cormier's novels are already familiar with Leominster, whether they realize it or not. They know the fictional town of Monument, Massachusetts, the setting of several of his novels, a town based on Leominster.

Cormier grew up in the French Hill section of town. The area was built in the early 1900s to accommodate laborers who were moving from Canada to work in Leominster's new comb factories. French Hill was home to immigrant workers of many nationalities including French, Italian, and Irish. Later, Cormier would describe this backdrop of his childhood as "a ghetto type of neighborhood" where "the streets were terrible."[4]

It was Robert Cormier's grandfather who brought the family to French Hill. He came to the United States to seek his fortune and soon owned an apartment building. "My grandfather [was] such a good man," recalled Cormier in 1972. "He owned what was probably the last horse team in town and would take his grandchildren for rides. It was a proud moment sitting beside him as he tugged the reins. . . . My grandfather was a cheerful man who liked horses and cowboy pictures and grandchildren."[5]

One son of this horse-loving, cheerful man was Robert's father, Lucien Joseph. Lucien was a factory worker in Leominster who met and married Irma Collins. The couple went on to create a family of eight children, of which Robert Edmund Cormier—born January 17, 1925—was the second. However, one of these children, three-year-old Leo, died when Cormier was five. Cormier recalled, "I was sort of his protector because we were close in age."[6] Along with the rest of his family, he mourned the loss of young Leo.

Young Cormier

Little Robert Cormier always dreamed of being a cowboy, specifically, a movie cowboy, but not one of those "who interrupted all the action to sing a song."[7] Later in life he would concede that he still dreamt of being a cowboy, but add that "it's ridiculous because . . . I'm not the outdoor type . . . [and] I've never even sat on a horse and know nothing about cows."[8]

Based on his admiration for movie cowboys it is not surprising that he and a childhood friend tried to make it to the Saturday afternoon cowboy movies at the Plymouth Theater every weekend. Cormier loved the movies and tried to emulate his favorite stars. He "would strut down the street like James Cagney or shrug [his] shoulders like John Garfield or take a drag on a cigarette like Humphrey Bogart."[9] When he was not at the movies, Cormier still had a great deal of fun. He and his friends spent their time playing "corner-lot" baseball, trading baseball cards, playing marbles, biking, trekking around Leominster, and figuring out ingenious ways to earn a little extra money to pay for ice cream and movies.

Their moneymaking schemes had to be fairly creative since Cormier was a boy during the Great Depression. He was four years old in 1929 when the stock market crashed. This crash further damaged the already weakened economy of the United States, and the country soon entered a time of severe poverty. The effects of this Great Depression were felt by many people well into the 1930s, and the citizens of Leominster, including the Cormier family, were no exception.

Although Cormier was only a child during the Great Depression, the period greatly influenced him. Cormier's father had to work a variety of jobs at the time, and many of these jobs were uncertain— here today, gone tomorrow. Watching Lucien struggle to feed and house his family made his young son admire and respect him. Lucien served as a very important role model in Robert's life. Over half a

Emulating movie stars like Humphrey Bogart (pictured) was a favorite boyhood pastime of Cormier.

century later Robert Cormier recalls, "my father . . . worked in a factory every day, never complained, took care of us even in the terrible days of the Great Depression."[10] He adds that during the time he learned a valuable lesson from observing his father, "if I wanted anything in life—success or just money in my pocket—I would have to earn it and not rely on others."[11]

The family also had to move frequently, although they always managed to remain in French Hill. In a 1976 newspaper article Cormier painted a picture of his childhood moving days:

> There was an old saying during the Depression that it was cheaper to move than to pay rent. My family was caught in the clutches of the Depression and we moved a lot . . . although my father always paid the rent.
>
> In those days tenements were plentiful and the physical part of moving was easy . . . people didn't move

The unemployed anxiously checked job postings during the Great Depression. Cormier's father also struggled to support his family during this devastating period.

far, only a street or two away. . . . Nobody ever saw a moving van on the streets of French Hill—friends and relatives and neighbors got together and did the moving, most often in a borrowed truck. There was a kind of carnival atmosphere to it all, especially when the men sat around afterward drinking home-brewed beer and marveling at the miracle of carrying that old black stove up three flights of stairs.[12]

Cormier describes his childhood self before entering high school as "a skinny kid" who "wasn't the physical type, the ball-playing type. . .[the kid who] never got chosen for the team."[13] Luckily Cormier seems to have worked out other arrangements: "In corner-lot baseball, I was secure in the knowledge that Pete [a childhood friend], who was a much better player, would choose me first."[14] The two boys were enrolled in St. Cecilia's School, a parochial school in French Hill that Cormier attended through eighth grade. In various interviews, Cormier expressed very complicated and mixed feelings about his time at St. Cecilia's. This was evident in an interview with Geraldine DeLuca and Roni Natov when Cormier stated that he had "a horrible time in parochial school and . . . also had a great time, you know?"[15]

Cormier was an avid reader. While other kids played, he could be found reading under the trees. Reading was his pastime and authors were his role models. "My heroes were in the library;" Cormier explained, "one of the greatest thrills of my life was when I graduated from the childhood section [of the library] to the adult section."[16] This was an honor that Cormier earned quite early, after he had read most of the children's books.

While Cormier worked his way through the library, he also made his way through St. Cecilia's. However, as his eighth grade graduation neared, misfortune struck the

Cormier family. Patricia Campbell described the incident in her book, *Presenting Robert Cormier:*

> On the morning of 10 June 1939 [Cormier] looked up from his schooldesk and glanced out the window, and there, across the street and beyond a vacant lot, his house was one solid sheet of flame. His mother and sister were home, he knew. He leaped to his feet in horror to run, but the teacher, a little bit of a nun who was a ferocious tyrant, cried "Wait! Bob, sit down! We're going to have some prayers before you run out!" And then while the flames crackled she forced him to take out his rosary and say a Novena . . . . When he was finally allowed to leave, he found to his relief that his mother and sister were safe, but the anger from the incident was a force in his life for many years.[17]

When he got home, he found that no one was hurt and once Cormier knew that everyone was safe, he "enjoyed the drama of firemen and fire trucks and howling sirens."[18] His family had to move and soon after Robert Cormier graduated from parochial school.

Following graduation, Cormier entered the local junior high for his ninth-grade year. It was around this time, when he was thirteen, that he read *The Web and the Rock* by Thomas Wolfe. Cormier credits this book with having "the greatest single effect on [him] as a writer." The book was about a small-town boy who wanted to be a famous writer. It helped Cormier realize that he was not alone; there were other people in the world who felt the same way he did. Reading it, Cormier said to himself, "That's me! I want to be a writer." [19]

In the months that followed, Cormier attempted to write in a style similar to that of Thomas Wolfe. But Wolfe's flowery style did not suit the young writer very well. The result was, in Cormier's words, "awful, terrible prose that [he] knew wasn't right."[20] Thus, although Cormier could appreciate the emotions that Wolfe conveyed and identify with the protagonist of *The Web and the Rock*, he did not model his writing style after Wolfe's. Instead, it was the simple and clear writing of Ernest Hemingway that influenced Cormier stylistically. Finally, Cormier maintains that a third author, William Saroyan, influenced the subject matter of Cormier's own work. Just as Saroyan wrote about everyday people in an Armenian neighborhood, Cormier would tell the stories of everyday folks in a French-Canadian one.

Life After High School

When Cormier graduated from Leominster High School in 1942, the United States was involved in World War II. Eighteen-year-old men across the country joined the armed forces, but the army rejected Cormier for service because of poor eyesight. Cormier explained his reaction:

I was devastated by my rejection by the army. You must understand the spirit of those days, how everybody wanted to fight the Japanese and the Germans. As president of my high school class, I thought of myself as a leader. Most of my class went for army induction together—and I was one of the few rejected.

Author Thomas Wolfe (pictured) influenced Cormier's early writing style.

I felt terrible about it. I tried twice more to enlist—at six-month intervals, and was turned down both of these times, too.[21]

Unable to join the army, Cormier went to work in a factory and, in 1943, he enrolled in evening classes at Fitchburg State College.

All the while, Cormier continued his writing. He worked on a short story about a U.S. soldier in World War II. The story centered around the soldier looking back on his life. Memories of family, friends, school, dances and numerous other things flooded the story. Then, it took a frightening twist as the reader realized that these were the soldier's thoughts in the final hour of his life—a final hour spent in a foxhole. The young man came to the conclusion that when he took stock of his life he didn't think of huge political events or anything such as that. Instead, he thought of these little things.

Cormier gave this story, titled "The Little Things That Count," to one of his college instructors, an art teacher named Florence Conlin. Without telling Cormier, she had the story typed and submitted it to a magazine called *The Sign*. They accepted it for publication and she came to Cormier's home excitedly waving a check. *The Sign* had paid seventy-five dollars for the story. When the May issue of the magazine appeared, Cormier was officially a paid, published author. He explained that this changed his family's perception of him: "Until then, I was that strange kid who was always in his room scribbling. But . . . as soon as you sell, you are a writer. My cousins and uncles and aunts who had thought that I was just a strange, eccentric little kid said, 'My God!, he made seventy-five dollars by putting words on paper.'"[22]

After a year at Fitchburg State College, Cormier left. Later, he accepted a job writing commercials for radio station WTAG in nearby Worcester, Massachusetts. Cormier called this "the worst experience of [his] work life" and added that "if you think commercials are terrible to listen to, they're awful to write."[23] Still, the job did help the young writer develop his skills. According to Cormier, he learned to write with great discipline "because the fellow who was paying for the commercial wanted to get in so much information, and I had only one hundred words in which to do it. This also taught me economy."[24]

Newsman and Family Man

Cormier soon married. He was still working at WTAG when he married Constance Senay. In her book, Campbell told the story of the couple's first meeting at a community dance:

> Bob loved to dance. First dance would always go to his sister Gloria, and then he would partner each of her girl friends in turn, spreading his favors around out of courtesy. One Saturday night Gloria arrived with her friend Constance Senay. Connie had been only a sophomore when Bob was a senior at Leominster High. He had been aware of her, but had never really paid any attention to the pretty French Hill girl whose mother ran the pharmacy. But politely he invited her to dance, and they stepped onto the floor together . . . he still gets starry-eyed when he describes the next moment. "She was fantastic! We just floated away!"[25]

After dating for a while, Robert and Constance were married on November 6, 1948.

Later that year, Cormier found the disciplined and economical writing style he learned while writing commercials came in handy when he took a job with a newspaper in Worcester. Cormier actively sought out a career in journalism because he "wanted to make [his] living at the typewriter"

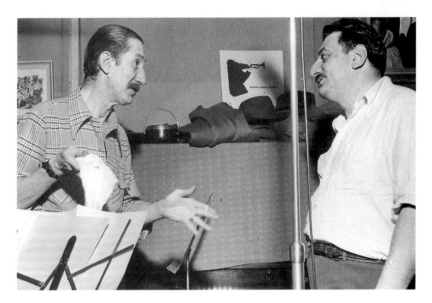

Listening to Pee Wee Russell (left) and other jazz greats inspired Cormier's first human interest story as a newspaper reporter.

and "journalism was a good way of earning [a] living working with words."[26] Thus, in 1948 he became a reporter for the *Telegram & Gazette.*

According to Cormier, his first story was not all that memorable and "probably a minor traffic accident." However, he remembers his first human interest story very well. It was titled "The Street of Music," and was about New York City's 52nd Street on which were located a series of bars where great jazz musicians played. Cormier sat and listened to "(now) old time greats Pee Wee Russell, Teddy Wilson, etc. . . . virtually all night long,"[27] then wrote about the experience. Cormier was now a journalist.

Three years later, Robert and Constance welcomed their first child into the world. Roberta Cormier was born in 1951; two years later, their son, Peter, followed. Then, in 1955, Cormier's employment situation changed. He moved from the *Telegram & Gazette* to its competition. Cormier was a new reporter for the *Fitchburg Sentinel & Enterprise* in the neighboring town of Fitchburg.

Cormier worked with the *Sentinel & Enterprise* in a variety of capacities for the remainder of his career in journalism. He started out as a reporter and in 1959 was promoted to wire editor for the paper. In 1964, he began writing a book review column followed by a human interest column named "And So On" in 1969. By the time he began this second column, he was already associate editor of the paper, a position he had taken in 1966. Over the course of his career at the *Sentinel & Enterprise*, Cormier won numerous awards for his work including an award given by the Associated Press in New England for best human interest story of the year. He won this award in 1959 and again in 1973.

A Novelist

As Cormier's journalism career flourished, his family continued to grow as well. He and Constance welcomed a third child, Christine, into the world in 1957. Everything was going well for the young Cormier family and then Cormier received some terrible news. His father Lucien had been diagnosed with lung cancer. "What is sad is what you cannot do," Cormier would later write. "You can't stop age from advancing on those you love or others for whom you have affection. You can't stop the years. You want to hold certain people at a certain moment of time forever but can't."[28]

As Cormier watched the painful process of his father dying, he began to write about it. It was his way of dealing with both his father's illness and death. Cormier later explained that he "wanted to put the whole world in bed with my father and—in a sense—kill them. I just wanted people to know that this man lived and died."[29] Eventually, Cormier was able to turn this painful incident in his life into art. Specifically, it became the foundation for his first novel, *Now and At the Hour.*

Now and At the Hour was published in 1960. This, Cormier's first novel, was written for an adult audience and told the story of a man coming to terms with his own death. It was an artistic beginning that Cormier had salvaged out of a painful ending in his own life. In the book, Cormier first explored some of the themes he would return to in his later novels. Now and At the Hour made critics aware of Cormier's talent. However, although the book enjoyed critical success, it sold relatively few copies.

Cormier's next two books were also for the adult audience. A Little Raw on Monday Mornings appeared in 1963 and two years later Cormier published his third adult novel, Take Me Where the Good Times Are. Critics appreciated both books, although neither received the critical acclaim that Now and At the Hour had. Cormier's next published novel, however, would have a great impact on many people, including critics. It would also stir up controversy in the world of young adult fiction.

J. D. Salinger (pictured), author of The Catcher in the Rye, first piqued Cormier's interest in writing fiction for adolescents.

Becoming an Author of Young Adult Fiction

In the late 1960s, Robert Cormier was a critically successful fiction author for the adult audience. He and his wife completed their nuclear family with a fourth child, Renee, in 1967. It was around this time that he discovered something about his children, namely, their lives had become more interesting than his own. "I found their lives exciting and tragic," said

Cormier, "a kid could go through a whole lifetime in an afternoon at the beach."[30] Cormier was also influenced by having read J. D. Salinger. *"The Catcher in the Rye* was a door-opener for me," Cormier said in a 1991 interview. "It made me see that adolescence could be something very dramatic to write about. Not that I sat down and said 'I'm going to write an adolescent novel' at the time . . . but it had a definite influence on me."[31]

Cormier began to write short stories about young people, stories that dealt with the problems they faced, as well as their relationships with parents and peers. These pieces appeared in magazines such as *Redbook, Saturday Evening Post*, and *McCall's*. Eventually, in 1980 some of these appeared in a collection of Cormier's short stories titled *Eight Plus One*.

After writing and publishing several short stories, Cormier believed the next logical step was a novel. He got an idea from the life of his son, Peter: Peter wanted to play football at school and was told that he needed to sell chocolates to raise money for the team. He already had enough to attend to with his schoolwork, and did not have the extra time to devote to chocolate sales. Cormier wrote a letter to the headmaster of his son's Catholic prep school asking that Peter be excused from the candy sale. The headmaster agreed, and while Peter was kidded good-naturedly by his classmates, all was well.

This incident started Cormier's creative wheels turning. He wondered "'What if?' What if the headmaster hadn't been understanding? And then, what if the chocolate sale was very important to his school? And then, what if he had peer pressure?"[32] His answers to these questions became the basis for the novel. After completing about a third of the book, Cormier sent it to his agent Marilyn Marlow. She was the first to suggest it might be a novel for a young adult audience.

The Chocolate War

Published in 1974, *The Chocolate War* was Cormier's first novel for young adults and caused quite a bit of controversy. It told the story of Jerry Renault whose refusal to sell chocolates at his private Catholic prep school did not end as nicely as Peter's had. Instead, Jerry's peers, as well as the headmaster and staff, mentally and physically tried to intimidate him into selling the chocolates. Jerry tried to stand up alone against this private school society, but they terrorized him. At book's end, Jerry was left defeated and wishing that he had never stood up to "Them," had never stood up for his beliefs.

Although critics appreciated Cormier's ability to tell the story, quite a few were concerned about what they perceived as the negativity and despair of the book's message. Since the great majority of young adult fiction ended happily or at least hopefully, some people were shocked by the book's tragic ending. Critics debated about the novel's overall message as well as whether it should be recommended for a teen audience. Essays, columns, and articles about the book abounded as they dealt with these issues.

At the same time the book was causing somewhat of a critical ruckus, it also caused a stir in local school districts. Some parents and teachers threatened to ban the book or require parental permission in order to read it. These would-be censors argued that the book was too disturbing and contained references to sex and violence. They also worried about some of the language.

In an article for *Catholic Library World*, Robert Cormier wrote about an attempt to remove *The Chocolate War* from the curriculum of a high school in a small town in Massachusetts. Students entering the ninth grade were assigned the book to read over the summer. Some parents and at least one School Board member objected to the use of the novel as a required assignment. A town hearing was called, the debate was aired in the local papers, and pandemonium ensued. In the end, there was a great deal of smoke, but very little fire. Those opposed to the book were revealed to be a very small minority and *The Chocolate War* remained part of the school's curriculum.

In the midst of this debate, young readers were some of Cormier's staunchest supporters. When Cormier visited the school, a teacher informed him that her students had circulated a petition in support of the book. In so doing, they also showed their understanding of the book's message. The teacher explained:

> One student stood up and said: "Everyone in this class should sign the petition." Another student stood up to say: "Wait. If we insist that everybody signs this petition, then we'd be doing what happens in *The Chocolate War*. Let's not pressure anybody to sign." . . . This thrilled [the teacher]. It made all the dispute and controversy worthwhile because the students had learned something from the novel and translated it into action.[33]

While most teachers and schools that used *The Chocolate War* had no trouble, there were other attempts to remove the book from the curriculum and libraries of schools. These were, however, the exception instead of the rule, and six years after publication, *The Chocolate War* had sold nearly half a million copies. The book introduced Robert Cormier to a teen audience and vice versa.

Subsequent Books

It has been more than a quarter of a century since *The Chocolate War* first appeared in bookstores. While it remains his most commercially successful book to date, in the years following its publication, Robert Cormier has continued to write both for young adults and children. *I Am the Cheese* came three years later. The success of this second young adult novel allowed Cormier to leave his job at the *Fitchburg Sentinel & Enterprise* and write full time.

He followed up *I Am the Cheese* with another somber novel, *After the First Death*, in 1979. A year later came the book of short stories titled *Eight Plus One*. Cormier told his readers that these stories were about "family relationships, fathers and mothers, daughters and sons . . . about growing up."[34] These lighter, happier works were something new and unexpected for Cormier's readers.

Cormier's fourth young adult novel, *The Bumblebee Flies Away*, appeared in 1983 and told the story of Barney Snow, a patient in an experimental hospital. That same year, a motion picture adapted from *I Am the Cheese* was released starring Robert Wagner. Two years later came a sequel to the book that first made a name for Cormier in young adult fiction: *Beyond the Chocolate War* was published in 1985. It blended a cast of returning characters with new ones, and readers finally had a chance to see some of the "bad guys" get what was coming to them in this one.

In 1988, Cormier published his last book of the decade, *Fade*. The story was about a boy who inherits the ability to make himself invisible. Cormier's work, on the other hand, was quite visible. *The Chocolate War* was released as a motion picture in 1989, and by the early 1990s Cormier had established himself as both a foremost writer of young adult fiction and a prolific one. The 1990s brought eight new Cormier titles. Cormier began the new decade by publishing a children's book titled *Other Bells Ring For Us*. A year later, in 1991, *We All Fall Down* appeared. It was a very thoughtful novel tackling difficult issues such as alcoholism, suicide, and random violence.

The following year Constance Senay Cormier edited a new Cormier book for young readers. It was a collection of some of Cormier's John Fitch IV columns, a human interest column that Cormier wrote for the *Fitchburg Sentinel & Enterprise*.

The book *I Have Words to Spend* gave young adults a look at a completely different side of Cormier. They now had the opportunity to read Cormier the journalist, the man who wrote about his paranoid fear that the "whatchamacallits" were taking over the world. On the book's heels came another young adult novel for Cormier.

Tunes for Bears to Dance To appeared in 1992; it told the story of a young boy named Henry who, after his brother's death, befriends a Holocaust survivor. At the same time, Henry is encouraged and coerced to be anti-Semitic. Although Cormier was dealing with racial issues, critics were disappointed with the novel. *Horn Book* wrote that the novel lacked "the power typical of Cormier's work, and the characters [were] disappointingly one-dimensional."[35] In 1995, however, *In the Middle of the Night* was published, and it expertly dealt with themes such as revenge, scapegoating, and a boy's search for a meaningful relationship with his father.

The adult Cormier found it thrilling to dip his hand into the waters of the Indian Ocean at the western tip of Perth, Australia, a place he had read about as a boy.

Cormier's young adult novel about a serial killer, a young runaway, and an aging cop came next. *Tenderness* appeared in 1997 followed by *Heroes: A Novel* in 1998. *Heroes* tells the story of a horribly disfigured World War II hero who decides to seek revenge on his enemy rather than return triumphantly home. In the fall of 1999, Cormier published *Frenchtown Summer* about a boy who is an observer, an outsider. The story concerns the boy's quest to understand his own father. Surprisingly, this new book ends hopefully.

The past ten years have been good to Cormier. He fondly remembers "traveling to places like London, Stockholm, New Zealand and, particularly, Australia, and meeting readers, realizing how alike people (especially teenagers) are." He adds that a "big thrill" for him was "dipping [his] hand into the Indian Ocean at the western tip of Australia in Perth, a place [he'd] read about as a child in school."[36] Memorable things have happened for Cormier at home as well. His children are now themselves parents and Cormier a grandfather. He enjoys "the frequent family get-togethers" as well as the "affection of people in [his] hometown who seem to share in [his] success."[37]

Today Cormier can be found in that hometown of Leominster living only three miles away from the house in which he was born. The city holds his past, his present, and most likely his future. "As we turn toward a new century," Cormier says, "I hope to go on writing every day, hear from my readers, [and] spend time with my friends and family."[38]

CHAPTER TWO

The Impact of the Novel

In order to comprehend the impact of Robert Cormier's work, it is first necessary to understand young adult fiction and its history. In the 1920s and 1930s book publishers began to separate books intended for youth from those written for adults. For the first time, they offered categories of fiction for children and young adults. This, in part, resulted from school and labor reforms of the early 1900s that gave more youngsters the chance to learn how to read. As more and more youth read and purchased books, more and more publishers created books for this new market.

Today, young adult fiction is generally defined as fiction that "readers between the approximate ages of twelve and twenty [willingly] choose to read."[39] While the ages sometimes vary according to different critics, this is a useful way of thinking about the category, or genre. Another way of thinking about the category is that young adult fiction is the "no-man's land" between books written specifically for children and books written for adults. These books tackle a lot of issues that children's books do not touch, but they are not written for the adult audience.

Donna Norton maintains that from the 1930s until the 1960s young adult books had many similarities. They depicted children in happy families and communities, and advocated religious values, respect for the law, and a strong patriotism. Norton adds that "unsurprisingly, given their secure lives . . . children in these books have few emotional problems."[40] The plots of these books revolved around adventure and issues such as popularity and dating. The problems were simple. Solutions abounded. Novels ended happily.

However, in the late 1960s a new kind of young adult novel started to gain in popularity. Called "problem novels," "realistic young adult fiction," or "New Realism" by critics, this new brand of young adult novel dealt with more serious issues. Authors wrote about suicide, drug abuse, divorce, and many other not-so-simple problems.

Even though these novels dealt with weightier issues, they generally had happy, or at least hopeful endings. Protagonists whose friends died found greater purpose and hope in their own lives; drug abusers received help; and young heroes and heroines learned to accept and to make the best of their divorced families. Although problems existed, Roger Sutton suggests, problem novels were usually "about *solutions* to those problems, and about the integration of the wayward (or waylaid) protagonist into responsible, adult society."[41]

In other words, these books dealt with the protagonist's search for a solution to, or a way to cope with, the problem. It ended when he or she found a solution. That novels written for teens should have hopeful endings and focus on personal development were two unwritten rules in the world of young adult fiction.

Cormier's *The Chocolate War*

When Robert Cormier tried his hand at writing young adult fiction he broke the mold. In 1974 he published *The Chocolate War*. This was his first novel for young people and it "departed from standard models and [broke] some of the most fundamental taboos"[42] of young adult fiction. For starters, *The*

Chocolate War broke the happy ending rule. It offered neither a solution, nor a way of coping with the problem that its protagonist, Jerry Renault, faced. There was no happy ending and no quick fix. Jerry, the "good guy," was completely defeated, his health in jeopardy at book's end. Moreover, he did not even achieve a moral victory. The book concluded with Jerry—who stood up against the evil system—believing he should have just gone along and gotten along as far as the chocolate sale was concerned. Essentially, all hope was lost.

Not only did *The Chocolate War* provide no solution, it also was not about Jerry's personal development. According to Anne Scott MacLeod, this was indicative of the second rule Cormier broke—while most books for teens were focused on personal development, his work was political. For example, in *The Chocolate War*, "Jerry's motivation for his lonely rebellion . . . is not dwelt upon at any great length."[43] The story focuses instead on how the private school society violates Jerry's rights, the rights of an individual.

The Chocolate War's focus on the political, combined with its unhappy ending, caused quite a stir in the world of young adult fiction. Critics praised Cormier's skillful writing, but argued over whether the book was suitable for young adults. Book reviewers cautioned parents about the downbeat ending and school boards contemplated banning the book for reasons such as language.

I Am the Cheese

While critics, parents, teachers, and school boards wrangled over *The Chocolate War*, Cormier began writing what would become *I Am the Cheese*. The germ of the idea seems to have come from his work in journalism. As an editorial writer, Cormier read a variety of newspapers and press releases. His reading made him aware of the extent to which the U.S. government was involved in the lives of its citizens. He also became, in his own words, "a little paranoid"[44] and believed that perhaps all people were just a little paranoid as well.

In a 1978 interview, Cormier explained the emotion he started with and tried to reproduce for his readers. "The phone clicks. I think twenty [now more than forty] years ago we'd have thought, 'Well, there's something wrong with the line.' Today, there's a click and you wonder. And if there's no click, you think, well, they're so sophisticated today, they can even listen without a click. So I wanted to portray [this] kind of fear that is in our lives today."[45]

Then, one day, after setting aside a sequel to *The Chocolate War* he had started, Cormier did a writing exercise. He "put a boy on a bike and had him take off on a Wednesday morning with a box on his bike."[46] Cormier asked himself questions, wondering why the boy was out of school, where he was going, what was in the box. He gave the boy many of his own fears and phobias. The character started to come alive.

According to Cormier, it was around this time that he "became aware of this alias [witness protection] program at a time when there wasn't too much publicity about it . . . I was just toying with this idea of what would happen to a boy in an alias program. And then one night I was sitting and I thought of the boy on the bike and it was almost like a bolt from the blue. I thought, suppose the boy was on the bike because of the alias program."[47] Thus, Cormier put all three components together: he knew he wanted to convey a fearful paranoia; he had the boy on the bike as character; and now he had the alias program for the plot. *I Am the Cheese* began to take shape.

When the book first appeared in 1977, the controversy surrounding *The Chocolate War* was still in the air. In 1974 Cormier had been an unknown in young adult fiction. Now, three years later, critics and readers awaited the publication of his second novel for the teen audience. Perhaps precisely because people had a better idea of what to expect from Cormier, *I Am the Cheese* had a very different impact than *The Chocolate War*.

The book's unhappy ending and political nature were less

shocking to reviewers. However, critics were surprised—some more pleasantly than others—by the fact that Cormier broke with a third accepted practice of young adult literature. In a category of fiction where narratives were typically straightforward, *I Am the Cheese* was extremely complex. The structure and style of the novel would change the way Cormier and others viewed the teen audience, and the commercial success of the work established Cormier as one of the foremost, and controversial, authors of young adult fiction.

Unhappy Endings and Politics

I Am the Cheese once again broke the happy ending rule of literature for youth. Critics immediately observed the book's ending was a "climax of depressing violence and a conclusion of almost intolerable despair."[48] One of very few critics who were outraged by this was Audrey Laski, who worried that the book "could do real harm to a disturbed adolescent, since it communicates all too effectively the paranoid fear that a psychiatric questioner may be an enemy—and then shows that it is true."[49] A few other critics cautiously recommended the book, warning parents that "sixteen is young enough" for children to read a book with such a "searing and horrifying"[50] conclusion. When readers and critics asked Cormier why his books ended so unhappily he answered simply that "the good guys don't always win."[51]

However, in order to understand what Cormier was trying to achieve with an unhappy ending, it is useful to review a more detailed response to this question, which he provided in a 1981 essay entitled "Forever Pedaling on the Road to Realism." In it, Cormier reveals that his original purpose for writing a novel is to create a fictional reality where readers *really* feel certain emotions. In the case of *I Am the Cheese*, he wants readers to feel the paranoia that Adam does. Cormier wrote that he starts with an emotion and then creates characters to help convey it to his readers. Once created, these characters became real. They have their own individuality and personality. At that point, Cormier argues, "you must follow the inevitability of [the characters'] actions. These actions determine the course and outcome of the novel."[52]

Cormier further explained that he does not believe that authors should manipulate characters to achieve a specific, perhaps happy, ending. For example, in *I Am the Cheese* Adam is a fearful teenager. He is locked in an institution and has little recollection of who he is or what he is doing. It would seem ridiculous if he suddenly came up with an extensive plan of escape requiring a great deal of courage, or if Aunt Martha showed up and they both lived happily ever after. Indeed, even Cormier himself even wishes there could be a happy ending for Adam, where he is free and happy, but adds that such an ending is "beautiful to contemplate . . . but not realistic, sad to say."[53] Thus, Cormier's first goal in writing a book is to convey an emotion through the realistic actions and reactions of his characters. In order to achieve this, he is willing to give up the happy endings he wishes he could write.

I Am the Cheese was also a political novel, thus breaking a second standard of young adult fiction. As was the case with *The Chocolate War*, the book was not really about the personal development of its protagonist, Adam Farmer. MacLeod suggests that "if we care about what happens to [Adam], it is not because of any crucial internal decision he must make, but . . . because he is the helpless victim."[54] She asserts that *I Am the Cheese* makes an even stronger political statement than *The Chocolate War* because "Cormier dispenses with metaphor. This stark tale comments directly on the real world of government, organized crime, large-scale bureaucracy, the apparatus of control, secrecy, betrayal, and all the commonplaces of contemporary political life."[55] Cormier himself admits that the book is "critical of government."[56] However, although critics such as MacLeod argued that *I Am the Cheese* was more political in nature and others called the ending even more unhappy, the book did not cause the uproar that Cormier's first teen novel had.

The Technique of *I Am the Cheese*

What quite a few critics did comment on was Cormier's writing and clever craftsmanship of *I Am the Cheese*. "A magnificent accomplishment," raved Paul Heins, "a brilliant technical tour de force . . . cunningly wrought, shattering in its emotional implications."[57] Newgate Callendar commended Cormier's "highly sophisticated style . . . and literary workmanship."[58] Some critics were pleasantly surprised by the effectiveness of the three intertwined narratives of the work. They explained to readers that at first they were concerned that this technique was going to be "difficult and pretentious,"[59] but found it worked. Margery Fisher put it succinctly, stating the "technique . . . added something positive and integral to the whole."[60]

While critics admired the book's complex structure, some also wondered if it might be too complicated for teens. One of the book's earliest reviewers wondered "will the style and, indeed, some of the actual content be above the heads of most teen-agers?"[61] Even Cormier himself wondered if this might be a problem. He was so concerned that the book was too complex that he sent the completed manuscript with an apology. It warned Fabio Coen, who had published *The Chocolate War*, "you've done this great thing in introducing me to this [young adult] audience and now I'm letting you down."[62]

However, what Cormier found instead was that "young readers . . . accepted *I Am the Cheese* even more than *The Chocolate War*" and that some young people were delighted to read "a book that is not written in one- or two-syllable words and [had] three different levels of development."[63] The teen-age readers' reception of *I Am the Cheese* led

Cormier to conclude that in his writing he "aimed for the intelligent reader and . . . often found that that reader is fourteen years old."[64]

Critics also appreciated the book as something substantial for young readers. They praised its complexity and plot in contrast to the run-of-the-mill book for the teen audience. *The Junior Bookshelf* told readers *I Am the Cheese* was "not another cozy tale for tired teenagers but a serious and challenging thriller of considerable merit."[65] Similarly, Lance Salway declared that "beside [*I Am the Cheese*], most books for the young seem as insubstantial as candyfloss."[66]

However, some critics were downright irate about the novel's complexity. *I Am the Cheese* caused reviewer Audrey Laski to wonder "why novels should be specially written for [young adult] readers at all" since "so few concessions [were] . . . made to the adolescent reader."[67] Laski longed for the time when one could at least count on the narrative mode of books for youth being straightforward, and found the narrative of *I Am the Cheese* "complex, and indeed irritating."[68]

Critical comments such as these highlight what was perhaps the most significant impact *I Am the Cheese* made on the world of young adult fiction. *The Chocolate War* with its unhappy ending and political message had already broken two significant rules of young adult fiction. *I Am the Cheese* broke these rules again, but it also broke a third. The complexity of *I Am the Cheese* expected a great deal more of young adult readers than did *The Chocolate War* and other books written for teens. It featured three intertwined narratives from numerous viewpoints. Readers had to make inferences, to piece together the logical puzzle. The critical and commercial success of the book seemed to indicate that young adults were both ready and willing to read more challenging books. This altered the way that authors, editors, publishers, and critics viewed the teen audience.

CHAPTER THREE

The Plot

In many ways Robert Cormier's *I Am the Cheese* is similar to a mystery novel. The central problem driving the plot of the book is the reader's attempt to figure out what happened, and where the protagonist Adam Farmer is as a result. This is indeed difficult to understand since Cormier presents the reader with "one genuine past, a set of events that happened and are now over, and what appear to be two different presents that the past has led to."[69] One present tells the story of Adam taking an arduous bike trip to see his father in Rutterburg, Vermont. The second present consists of taped conversations between Adam and Brint—who may or may not be a doctor. The reader not only needs to figure out what happened in the past, but also must resolve the two presents. Basically, the first-time reader attempts to discern which present came first, since it is difficult to believe that Adam can simultaneously be on a bike trip to Rutterburg and having a conversation with Brint. The story unfolds as Cormier jumps back and forth between the two presents, all the while giving the reader clues about the past.

Two Presents

The book begins with someone—only later is his name revealed to be Adam—setting out on a bike trip. He retrieves pants, shoes, a jacket, and his father's old cap from the cellar, raids his savings, and throws away his pills. Adam's old-fashioned bike is difficult to pedal, but he is determined to ride it to Rutterburg,

Vermont, to visit his father. In the front basket he carries a package wrapped safely for his dad. Adam did not say goodbye to anyone before he left—not even Amy, a yet unidentified character. He glances back over his shoulder to make certain that no one is following him as he starts on his bicycle journey.

The next chapter is a transcript of a taped session between Brint—whose dialog is labeled with the letter T—and someone whose dialog is labeled A—later he is also revealed to be Adam. This session is being recorded as part of the TAPE OZK series. Brint asks Adam to tell him about "that night." Adam remembers when he was about three and a half he woke up from a nightmare and heard his parents speaking "louder and harsher" than usual. They worried he would hear their conversation so he listened all the more intently as they discussed what to do about him. They said he was too young to understand, then he heard them begin discussing a trip they would all take together.

Adam tells Brint the trip was an endless journey on a bus, the mood of which was "spooky, scary . . . as if we were being chased." When Brint asks more questions Adam hesitates, not knowing why. He does not entirely trust Brint and wonders whether he should tell him about the clues. Brint eagerly jumps on the word "clues" and Adam suspects his medication is playing tricks on him—making him believe he is only thinking when he is really speaking aloud. Overcome by panic, he decides to be very careful from here on out. Their session ends.

The book then returns to Adam the bike rider. He is at a gas station looking at a map and discussing his trip with the attendant. Adam will have to travel seventy miles in order to reach Rutterburg. Adam worries that the attendant will ask about his parents, but he does not. Instead, he gives Adam the map and Adam is on his way again.

The conversation between Brint and Adam continues in the following chapter. Brint asks whether Adam wants to dis-

cuss Paul Delmonte or Amy Hertz. Instantly Adam is overcome with a headache, anxiety, and nausea. Their conversation
is suspended.

Meanwhile, the bike trip continues and Adam is riding
along and singing "The Farmer in the Dell" in the same way
his father (David) always sings it. When he was young his
father joked that it was written just for them since their last
name was Farmer. For the first time the reader learns that the
bicyclist's name is Adam Farmer.

Growing Fears

In the next chapter Brint is asking many questions, but Adam
is verbally unresponsive. However, he is thinking about Brint
and wondering if he is a doctor. Adam thinks that sometimes
looking in Brint's eyes is like looking down the barrel of a gun.
Brint decides to postpone their talk since he is receiving no
response.

Adam's bike trip becomes treacherous when he confronts
a German shepherd. He pedals faster to get by, but the dog
attacks, biting the front tire and trying to topple the bike.
Finally, a car happens by and the dog takes off to chase it
instead. Adam makes it into the town of Fairfield and should
stop—he is tired and has to use the bathroom—but instead he
keeps going to escape the dog that he fears will follow him forever.

In their conversation, Adam asks Brint if he is a doctor and
whether "this" is a hospital. Brint asks Adam what he thinks
and Adam concludes that the place is similar to a private sanitarium. Brint wants to begin their conversation again and
while Adam realizes he is distrustful of Brint, he does not say
anything. He supposes he has no rational, concrete reason to
distrust Brint and decides to proceed cautiously and cunningly, to tell him about some—but not all—of the clues.

The first clue Adam discusses is the dog. Brint asks if he
means Silver, a German shepherd at the hospital and Adam says

he means some other dog. He then recalls a day when he was nine years old. He and his father were walking to the library when his father stopped abruptly, looked terrified, and tugged Adam into the woods (for the first time the person talking to Brint has memories of being called Adam). Once again, as in the case of the bus trip, Adam had the feeling that they were being chased. Suddenly, a growling dog stood in front of them and Adam's father successfully fended off the dog.

Brint urges Adam to explain why he believes this piece of the past is a clue. Adam tells him at the time the immediate danger of the dog overshadowed his father's panic and flight into the woods. However, the incident was important in retrospect because Adam felt once again that his father was running from something.

Amy Hertz

On his bike trip Adam stops to try to call Amy Hertz but decides it's too early and she will not be home from school. Later, he tries and the phone rings, but no one answers. Adam concludes that it is still too early for her to be home from school.

In their session, Brint asks about Amy Hertz. He wants to know if she was just a friend or more. Adam says she was more than a friend. He remembers first meeting her and falling in love with her right then and there. Soon after, Amy began to take him on Numbers. The basic Number was going to the grocery store, filling up shopping carts and leaving them around the store. However, Amy was extremely creative and the two began to do a variety of Numbers the goal of which was to confuse people and make a scene. One day after a particularly funny and successful Number, Adam took Amy home and kissed her. She was the first girl he had ever kissed and he loved her.

Adam tells Brint that Amy is a clue because she phoned him "that afternoon." Amy and Adam were close so he told her about his childhood—that he had moved to Monument when he was four from a small town called Rawlings,

Pennsylvania. One day Amy called from her father's newspaper office. An editor from Rawlings was visiting and Amy had mentioned the Farmers, wondering if he knew Adam's parents. The man stated that he had lived in Rawlings his whole life, knew everyone in town, but could not remember any Farmers ever living there. When Amy asked, "Didn't you say you were born there?" he remembered the frightening bus ride and then lied to Amy without knowing why. Adam tells Brint that after this conversation he felt funny, as though something were wrong. Adam doesn't want to talk anymore and is beginning to remember everything. The session ends.

Two Identities

Rain interrupts Adam's bike trip. He huddles under a tree for shelter, takes his father's package off the bike, and hugs it to keep it dry. As the rain pours down Adam sings "The Farmer in the Dell" and resolves to continue on to Rutterburg.

In their next conversation, Brint declares that Adam has reached the point (in remembering his past) where his suspicions were aroused. Adam doesn't remember ever arriving at that point, but continues on. Adam admits that although he suspected that something was wrong after the phone call, he didn't confront his parents. Instead, he began to look for other information to either confirm or dispel his suspicions. His search led him to break into the bottom drawer of his father's desk where all the important papers were kept. In the drawer he found two different birth certificates for himself. One had the correct birthday; however, in a sealed envelope he found a second birth certificate. The second birth certificate had the wrong birth date written on it. This find made him tremble and shake. Adam assumed that there must be a reasonable explanation—why would he have two birth certificates?—but he wondered.

Even though Adam has a headache and wants to stop talking, Brint presses on, asking about this discovery. After he found the two birth certificates, Adam began to examine the everyday routine of his home life. This called his mother's Thursday night phone calls into question. Brint wants to know about the calls, but Adam is becoming more suspicious. He says he has a feeling Brint already knows everything, even Adam's blank spots. Brint continues questioning him and Adam becomes a bit rebellious, refusing to offer the information to Brint. He is tired and dislikes Brint because he asks too many questions. In the end, however, Adam gives in and discusses the calls.

Adam wondered to whom she spoke. She was not on any committees, didn't have any friends, and his parents said they had no living relatives. One Thursday night he listened in on his mother's call and heard her talking to her sister, his aunt. He did have a living relative. For the first time, he realized his parents had been lying to him his entire life. Brint asks what Adam did with this information, but Adam is ill—dizzy and nauseated. They end their session.

The Troublemakers

The biking Adam is taking a little breather. He stops at a lunchroom in Carver for a bite and encounters three trouble-makers—Dobbie, Lewis, and Whipper. The three wise guys begin harassing Adam. When Whipper spots the package Adam is carrying for his father, he threatens to open it. Adam stands up to Whipper, who eventually backs down and allows Adam to leave the lunchroom.

Brint is called at 2:15 A.M. to continue the conversation. Adam awoke from a nightmare wondering "who is Adam Farmer?" Adam asks Brint a barrage of questions that Brint cleverly turns back on him. Finally, Adam's panic subsides—without Brint saying much—and Adam returns to his room to sleep.

Adam is ready to leave Carver on his bike when he decides to try to call Amy. A grumpy man answers the phone and it is not Amy's father. From inside the phone booth Adam sees the three troublemakers approaching and he worries that the bike is sitting unlocked, vulnerable. Realizing he has the wrong number, Adam apologizes and hangs up the phone, and gets out of the phone booth. He jumps on the bike and barely escapes the wise guys as he quickly pedals out of town.

In his conversation with Brint, Adam mentions the gray man who he knows is a clue. He is on the verge of remembering and Brint tells him to relax so the memory can come. Brint suggests they talk about something else in the meantime, perhaps Paul Delmonte. Adam asks if Paul is the gray man and then suddenly decides not to say another word. The session is suspended.

As Adam pedals his bike about a mile outside of Carver he thinks about Amy. Then, he hears a car coming. The troublemakers from the lunchroom are in the car. They circle around Adam in their car, harassing him; finally, a car passes and the people in the car—it is unclear whether or not it is the troublemakers—reach out and push Adam into a ditch. He hears them laughing.

Secrets Revealed

The next two chapters show Brint questioning Adam. He is worried that Adam is not eating or sleeping. He is only lying in bed and staring at the ceiling. Adam does not respond to Brint. In the second of the chapters, Brint is encouraged that Adam looks better and has eaten, but Adam is still unresponsive and Brint is forced to end their session.

Adam lies by his bike in the ditch. A voice asks him whether he is all right and he is able to stand up. Adam accepts a ride to Hookset from an elderly couple named Arnold and Edna. Hookset is just outside Belton Falls where Adam plans to stay for the night before continuing on to Rutterburg in the morning. In the car, Adam falls asleep singing "The Farmer in the Dell" and when they reach their destination Arnold wakes him up, drops him off, and wishes him luck.

The book returns to Adam and Brint who are talking again. Adam is complaining that his body hurts where all the needles poked him. Brint insists that the medications were all necessary since Adam had "retreated completely." Adam admits that he doesn't understand why he's "there," or how he got "there." Brint assures him that this information is what they are attempting to learn together.

Adam reveals that he now knows who the gray man is. The gray man was a part of their lives, commonplace. His name was Mr. Grey and he came to the Farmer house once or twice a month. Adam was told he was the supervisor of the New England branch of the insurance company for which his father worked.

After his discovery of the secret aunt, Adam became suspicious of Mr. Grey's visits. One day when Mr. Grey was over he decided to eavesdrop. He didn't hear anything, but his father saw him (although he didn't let on at the time). Later, Adam overheard his parents—who thought he was away—discussing him. They "whispered frantically" about his spying. They had noticed he listened in on his mother's conversation and eavesdropped on Mr. Grey (or Thompson as they were now supposed to call him). After hearing them, Adam finally asked his father to tell him what was going on. His father revealed that his name was not really Adam Farmer, it was Paul Delmonte. Brint asks what else his father told him and Adam says "almost everything."

Adam learned that his father's real name was Anthony Delmonte. After getting an advanced degree in journalism, he had returned to his hometown of Blount, New York, to work for the local newspaper, the *Telegrapher*. His love of journalism and talent soon earned him awards and a promotion to political writer for the paper; sometimes he even covered political events in the state capital of Albany. During this time, Anthony met and married Louise Nolan. Soon Louise gave birth to their son, Paul, and "life was good." Brint seems impatient and Adam becomes suspicious. He tells Brint that sometimes he wonders what's more important, Adam learning about his past, or Brint learning about it.

Despite his doubts Adam continues to answer Brint's questions—why had the Delmontes left Blount? Adam's father said that their lives changed forever when he uncovered incriminating documents while reporting from the state house in Albany. Brint wants to know what kind of information Adam's father found. Adam says that it connected the local, state, and federal governments to organized crime. Brint wants him to be more specific about this information. This makes Adam even more suspicious that Brint is after information and not really out to help him.

He tells Brint that his father felt it was his duty as a citizen of the United States to do his part. Therefore, he testified against many powerful men under the condition that his name be kept secret, otherwise his life would be in danger. Brint suddenly asks why Adam said earlier that his father had told him almost everything. Adam tells him his father didn't give him certain information for his own protection. Brint is curious about this untold information and questions Adam about it. Adam is very confused by Brint's questioning—it's as though Brint wants him to betray someone.

Enter Mr. Grey

Brint redirects the conversation and begins asking about Anthony's testimony. Adam says that for about a year his father was away from his family, testifying and living in hotel rooms. Finally the trial was over and he went home. Following his return, the Blount police were alerted to a bomb planted on the Delmonte family car. Luckily, they disarmed it and no one was hurt. A few days later, Anthony was coming home from work when a hit man dressed as a police officer raised his gun and aimed to shoot. Anthony thought his life would end, but instead the hit man was shot.

That was the night that Mr. Grey entered their lives. Mr. Grey was one of the founders of the U.S. Department of Re-Identification and he encouraged Anthony to enter their witness protection program. Anthony hesitated, but changed his mind when Louise received a threatening phone call declaring that two funeral masses—for Anthony and Paul—had been reserved for the next week. Anthony agreed to enter the program.

Thus, they became the Farmers. Anthony became David; Louise kept her name; and Paul's name was changed to Adam. They were relocated to Monument, Massachusetts. Brint asks why Monument and Adam says Brint sounds bored, as if he's already heard this all before. He tells Brint that Monument was chosen because it was on the East Coast—the Delmontes would blend in. Adam adds that there was very little chance of anyone ever tracing them back to Blount since Mr. Grey arranged for it to appear as though the Delmontes had been killed in a car accident. This memory upsets Adam and Brint suspends the session for the day.

Friends and Enemies

After being dropped off in Hookset, Adam had gone into the drugstore and when he re-emerges, his bike is gone. He searches for it and encounters a heavyset man named Arthur who eventually tells him that Junior Varney has stolen his bike.

In their next session Brint continues questioning Adam about the incriminating information that Anthony uncovered. Adam becomes extremely suspicious and notes that Brint is looking at him as though he is his enemy. Although Brint tries to allay Adam's fears, Adam is now convinced that Brint is not a doctor at all and fears that he is an enemy. Even so, he realizes that he is completely dependent on Brint in order to regain his past and reclaim his life.

He asks Brint why he never inquires about his mother. Brint tells him to talk about his mother if he wishes. Adam tells Brint that she thought they trusted Mr. Grey too much, and that she was more rebellious than his father and sometimes broke the rules on purpose. It was his mother who took him back to the past once. They went down into the basement and she showed him some things she had saved—against Grey's wishes—from their old life. This included some of Adam's baby things, a jacket, a green scarf, and an old cap of his father's (the same clothes Adam is wearing on the bike trip). Amy rang the doorbell and startled Adam and his mother while they were in the basement. She and Adam went to do a Number and Adam wanted desperately to tell her what was going on, but he couldn't—it was life or death. Adam suddenly stops his reminiscing and asks Brint where his parents are. Brint quickly rings to get him medication and tells him he must calm down. He ends the session for the day.

Adam's bike trip is momentarily stalled as he is forced to try to retrieve his bike. Adam thinks of himself as a spy as he stands across the street from Junior Varney's house watching and waiting for Junior to appear. When Junior comes out, Adam confronts him, saying he wants his bike back. The two wrestle over the bike, but it is Adam who is victorious. He rides out of town on the bike.

Adam tells Brint that he does not think that he is a doctor. Brint discusses it with him—cunningly revealing little—and suggests they discuss Amy. He asks whether Adam ever shared his knowledge with her. He did not, but desperately wanted to do so. The information and the fact that he couldn't share it made him avoid her. The last time he saw her, the Number they attempted failed; when they parted Amy had said, "Call me." Adam returned home to find his mother waiting for him. Grey had called. It was an emergency.

Adam hesitates to tell Brint more because he knows that he is a predator, an enemy, but he also needs him to understand his past. He recalls the emergency: the Farmers had to leave town, at least for a few days; Grey's men had heard Blount mentioned in a wire tap.

One Mystery Solved

On his bike trip, Adam finally reaches Belton Falls. He is excited to stay at the Rest-A-While Motel where he and his parents once stayed together. When he gets there, the motel is deserted. He and his parents were there just last year, but the place looks as though it has been deserted much longer. Adam tries to call Amy again and the same grumpy man answers the phone. There is no Amy. Adam confirms that he is calling the correct number and he is. The man says he has had it for three years. Adam hangs up the phone and calls directory assistance to locate Amy, but there is no listing for her in Monument. Adam asks a gas station attendant how long the motel across the street has been closed. When the attendant tells him it's been two or three years, Adam realizes that more time has passed than he can account for. He crosses the street and pounds on the cabins, screaming.

Adam tells Brint that the trip with his parents began as an adventure. They all sat together in the front seat of the car and sang "The Farmer in the Dell." They stopped for the night in Belton Falls and stayed at the Rest-A-While Motel. The next morning they set out again. His father suddenly remarked that they were being followed. He was certain it was Grey's men, that "he'd know them anywhere." Later, they all got out of the car to stretch their legs and a car smashed into them. Adam saw his mother die instantly. He heard a voice say his father had gotten away and another voice say they would catch him. Adam tried to get up from the pavement to see who it was and it was "him." Brint pushes Adam to give a name, but Adam only remembers his voice, gray pants, and him saying that his mother was "terminated, check the boy." Brint wants to know who it was, but Adam cannot respond. For the reader, the mystery of the past—what happened—is solved, but the relationship between the biking Adam and the Adam who talks to Brint is still unknown.

Putting the Pieces Together

The next chapter resolves these two presents. When Adam rides his bike into what he calls the town of Rutterburg, it slowly becomes apparent to the reader that he has only been cycling around the hospital grounds. All the characters he saw on his trip—Arthur, Junior Varney, Luke, Whipper, Dobbie, Lewis, and the German shepherd—are there. The two presents occurred simultaneously; one—the bike ride—was imaginary. A nice doctor, Dr. Dupont, takes Adam back to his room. Adam asks if his father is dead and he knows that his mother is. Dr. Dupont looks at him sadly. Adam begins to sing "The Farmer in the Dell." The doctor gives him medicine and opens the package; inside is Pokey the Pig. Adam continues rocking, holding Pokey and singing the last verse of "The Farmer in the Dell"—the cheese stands alone. He wonders who Paul is and can't remember the name Adam. He declares that he knows who he is; he is the cheese.

The book then further clarifies Adam's present situation. It is Brint's annual report on Adam for Department 1-R. He states that this third interrogation—each done at twelve-month intervals—was consistent with the first two. Brint asserts that Subject A (Adam) has no knowledge of the incriminating information his father knew, or who killed them. The report also states that the suspension of Personnel #2222 (Mr. Grey) should be discontinued since there is only circumstantial evidence to suggest that he was responsible for the deaths of Adam's parents (implying that Adam's father was indeed caught and killed the day of the crash). Finally, the report advises that Adam remain in confinement until either they kill him or he dies.

The final chapter of the book is one paragraph, the same paragraph that started the book. It suggests that Adam will simply begin this entire painful process again and again and again. . . .

CHAPTER FOUR

The Cast of Characters

Major Characters

Brint (last name unknown, a.k.a. "T")

Brint enters *I Am the Cheese* in taped sessions with Adam, stating that his name is Brint, and leaving the reader to wonder why he is identified on the transcripts as "T." Cormier admits this was done because he "wanted the reader to know right from the beginning: games are being played here, probably deadly games."[70] Also, it is important to realize that Cormier carefully chose the name Brint for this character. He wanted it to rhyme with flint and glint so as to "suggest someone bloodless and cold."[71]

On the first reading of the book Brint seems sympathetic, friendly, and as though he might even be trying to help Adam—that is, until the last few chapters. However, once the reader knows Brint's agenda, it is the cool, calculating representative of the system who comes into view. He may or may not actually be a licensed psychiatrist. Whether or not he is, he does seem to have a grasp of the vocabulary of mental health professionals and uses it to get Adam to trust him. Whenever Adam becomes suspicious and asks questions, Brint quickly turns Adam's questions back on him using this psychiatric vocabulary. In so doing, he is able to delay Adam's realization that Brint is an enemy. However, eventually Brint's eyes and questions give him away.

Brint is a representative of the cold, heartless system as well as the passive evil it produces, an evil that occurs when individuals do not question the morality of the system for which they work. Employed by his organization to find out whether Adam has knowledge of either the content of Anthony Delmonte's testimony (File Data 865-01) or who killed his parents, for the past three years Brint has gone to work, leading Adam on an annual journey to relive his parents' murder. Brint would recommend that Adam's life also be terminated, if only the current organizational bylaws allowed it.

Dressed in a spiffy suit and tie—unlike the doctors and nurses—Brint is a drone; he never questions the organization he works for, one that psychologically tortures and would murder a teenage boy. He has no sympathy for Adam or qualms about his line of work. Instead, he dutifully does his job. Always on call, available at 2:15 A.M. when needed, he is the ideal employee. He rarely seems to display human emotion and when he does, it is usually a line he is feeding Adam to gain his trust. Brint obviously takes his job very seriously and unquestioningly.

Adam Farmer (a.k.a. Paul Delmonte, Subject A)

A shy and insecure teenager, Adam (Paul Delmonte) is the unsuspecting, unlikely and tragic hero—perhaps victim—of *I Am the Cheese*. The son of David and Louise Farmer (Anthony and Louise Delmonte), when his parents are murdered he becomes the last remaining link to File Data 865-01. Adam does not remember his past and the book unfolds as he, now seventeen years old, searches for it both on the bike ride and in conversations with Brint. At the same time, Brint is trying to discover whether Adam does indeed know the information contained in File Data 865-01, as well as who murdered his parents. If Brint determines that Adam has information about either, Adam will be "terminated."

Adam is a loner, an outsider. He would rather hang out reading and listening to old records than play with other kids.

He contends he is always an outsider—watching the other kids play games—by choice, that he never feels left out. He believes that being a loner is his basic nature—to be an observer, recording events, but not participating in them. A budding writer, Adam dreams of being the next Thomas Wolfe.

While Adam may be an observer by nature, the fact that he is painfully shy contributes to his being an outsider. He admits that this shyness prevents him from making friends and doubts his capability for intimacy with others. He has trouble telling potential friends about himself for fear that they will laugh or that he will lessen himself in their eyes. This is true even with Adam's only friend and first love, Amy Hertz. He does tell her some of his dreams, but cannot express his worries, doubts, or emotions to her because he fears she will laugh.

Adam thinks of himself as a coward and says he is "afraid of a thousand things, a million."[72] Yet, while he is constantly mentioning things that frighten him, he shows bravery in numerous situations. Riddled with his fears as well as headaches and stomach trouble, he is an average person forced by his circumstances to be a hero.

In *I Am the Cheese,* Adam represents the innocent individual who fights against systems. He is an all-American teenage boy with insecurities, ambitions, dreams, and a first love. From the outset of their conversations Adam is wary of Brint and does not know whether to trust him. In the end, Adam's innocence is used against him and eventually destroyed by Brint and the system he works for.

David Farmer (a.k.a. Anthony Delmonte, Witness #599-6)
David Farmer (Anthony Delmonte) was born and raised in Blount, New York. After completing his high school education, Anthony attended Columbia University and graduate school in Missouri. There, he received his graduate degree in journalism and returned to Blount to work for the *Telegrapher.* Over the years, he won awards and soon became a political writer.

During his time at the *Telegrapher*, Anthony met and married Louise Holden. The happy couple bought a house and had a child, Paul Delmonte (Adam Farmer). Soon after Paul was born, Anthony discovered some incriminating evidence while reporting on the events at the state house in Albany, New York. This information (File Data 865-01) connected various politicians at the local, state, and federal levels to organized crime. It also changed the course of his entire family's life.

Anthony "was an old-fashioned citizen who believed in doing the right thing for his country"[73] and so agreed to testify. As a result of this testimony, as well as the government's inability to keep his name from getting to the wrong people, attempts were made on his and his family's lives. In order to protect his wife and child, Anthony entered the U.S. Department of Re-Identification, a witness protection program, as Witness #599-6. He and his family were given new identities and became the Farmers.

David Farmer represents the individual trying to do the right thing for his society. He had to completely trust his government, to put the lives of himself and his family in their hands. However, his efforts are futile and fail to eradicate the evil, or even make much of a difference—he has only cut off one branch of the evil; all the others continue to grow. Meanwhile, he must give up many things he loves and eventually his life.

Louise Farmer (a.k.a. Louise Nolan, Louise Holden, Louise Delmonte)
Although Louise kept the same first name, she has more last names than any other character in the book. She was originally Louise Holden and then married Anthony Delmonte to become Louise Delmonte. When she entered the witness protection program, they gave her both a fake married name—Louise Farmer—and a fake maiden name—Louise Nolan. Critics have suggested that the last name Holden may be Cormier's tip of the hat to J. D. Salinger's *Catcher in the Rye*, especially because—like Holden

Caufield, Salinger's protagonist—she represents lost innocence. However, Cormier says her name "was not inspired by *The Catcher in the Rye*" but adds that "there are subconscious things working in my writing and this could be one of them."[74]

Her mother died giving birth. Her father was "seduced" by alcohol and passed out in an alley one winter night only to freeze to death, leaving Louise and her older sister, Martha, orphans. Despite all of this, Louise managed to remain happy, partly through her devout Catholicism and partly because she fell in love with Anthony Delmonte, married him, and had a child, Paul. When Adam (Paul) remembers his early childhood, his mother is full of laughter and tenderness, and always smells of lilac perfume. However, this happiness and innocence was short-lived.

The family's entrance into the government witness protection program transformed Louise into a very different woman, a "pale and subdued and antiseptic woman who seldom left the house, who lurked behind window curtains."[75] Throughout his childhood, Adam thought of her as sad and weak like "a faded color." Once he knows the truth, he realizes that his mother is very strong. The sad weakness he had felt growing up was actually more fearfulness. What Louise called Never Knows—never knowing what was going to happen, whether her husband or son would be hurt, or who their enemies and friends were—transformed the happy, carefree, innocent Louise into a frightened, cynical, angry, and sad woman. She lost her innocence and her happiness.

Louise is more defiant about their situation than Anthony. She rebels in small ways in an attempt to reclaim some portion of her carefree, happy life—a life without the Never Knows. She does not like, or altogether trust, Mr. Grey. After he learns the truth, Adam is delighted to find out Louise is not the sad, compliant mother he thought she was. Instead, she is angry and deceptive.

Mr. Grey (first name unknown, a.k.a. Thompson, Agent #2222)

Mr. Grey is a frightening form of evil. He has many names, is faceless, and is "so commonplace that he [is] invisible."[76] Mr. Grey works for the federal government; he is one of the original men involved with the U.S. Department of Re-Identification. After Anthony Delmonte's testimony, Mr. Grey implored him to let his family take part in the witness protection program his department offered. He gave Anthony, Louise, and Paul new names and papers. He arranged for it to appear that they had died in a car accident, and then relocated them to Monument as the Farmer family.

Adam describes Mr. Grey (or later, Thompson) saying "there was something—gray about him. His hair was gray. But more than that: to me, gray is a nothing color and that's how Mr. Grey seemed to me. Like nothing."[77] Indeed, Mr. Grey is an enigma and no one seems to know whether or not to trust him. David, Louise, and Adam all struggle with this. Even the Department 1-R is unsure whether Grey is trustworthy; still, in the end they have no hard evidence that he was involved in the death of Adam's parents and he is reinstated as an agent.

Mr. Grey is the destroyer of innocence as well as life. His rules and department transform Louise from a happy woman to a paranoid, sad one. She doesn't trust Grey and it is his rules she rebels against in an attempt to regain some form of happiness, even for a moment. It is unclear at the end of the book whether Mr. Grey did turn against Anthony Delmonte, but it certainly seems to be the case since Anthony seems confident that Grey's men were following the family just prior to the fatal accident. Thus, it appears that Grey's actions may have caused the death of Adam's parents, which in turn caused the loss of Adam's innocence.

The most frightening thing about Mr. Grey is that he represents an evil that is not easily identified and eradicated. He could be anyone, anywhere, at any time. Adam alludes to this when he first describes Mr. Grey to Brint. He tells Brint of a murder story in which "the cops were all watching the street, waiting for the killer to arrive, to strike. And the killer did arrive but nobody saw him. Later on, they discovered that the killer was the mailman, he had calmly walked down the street and no one had noticed him because he was like part of the scenery . . . That's the way the gray man was in our lives."[78]

Amy Hertz

Amy's name was also carefully chosen by Cormier. Her last name is Hertz, which sounds like "hurts." Cormier knew that "when he introduced her that she would have the power to hurt Adam."[79] She does not hurt Adam—Cormier emphatically denies that she has anything to do with Adam getting hurt—but this suggests Adam's love for her and his vulnerability. She is a fast-talking, mischievous, creative, and funny young girl; the moment Adam meets Amy Hertz he falls in love with her. When discussing their first meeting with Brint, Adam describes her as "short and robust and freckled, and one of her front teeth was crooked, but her eyes were beautiful, blue, like the blue of his mother's best china. She also had wonderful breasts."[80]

Amy is the child of the editor of the local paper and a woman obsessed with committee work. She is outgoing with Adam, calling attention even to things that embarrass her such as farting or her breasts. However, she also has a serious side. She isolates herself in the library for hours, listens to Adam's love poetry, and shows a genuine understanding of, and caring for, Adam throughout the book. Amy is pure good, a wonderful bright spot in Adam's otherwise tragic life. She is separate from all the intrigue, fear, and evil. Actually, she is the only person who can take Adam's mind off his doubts and troubles. She is also his only friend and the sole person whom he tells about his dreams. Later, he also draws strength from the possibility of talking to her and her memory on his bike trip.

It is Amy's phone call and inquiry into Adam's past as well as his instinctual answers that shift Adam's search for the truth into high gear. Amy is also the mastermind behind the Number—a prank invented and performed in order to make others (especially adults) wonder what happened. The Numbers she creates are actually quite harmless—filling shopping carts in supermarkets and abandoning them, turning hotel *Do Not Disturb* signs to *Please Make up the Room Early*. However, it is Adam's participation in them that convinces him he is "capable of mischief" and gives him the courage to start down the path of discovering his parents' secret.

Minor Characters

There are a great many characters in *I Am the Cheese* who are residents in the home and also appear in Adam's imaginary bike ride. Some of these characters try to help Adam, others attempt to stop him from visiting his father. While they appear very briefly and little is known about them, understanding both the characters and their actions is essential to comprehending *I Am the Cheese*.

Arnold and Edna (last name unknown)

Arnold and Edna are an elderly couple who find Adam in a ditch and give him a ride to Hookset on his imaginary bike trip. Unlike many of the others who appear on Adam's imaginary bike trip, Arnold and Edna do not reappear at the private home later in the book. This is most likely because they are driving in for a doctor's appointment and do not live at the home.

Arnold is a kind old man with a "grandfather kind of face"[81] and a Yankee twang who finds Adam in the ditch where Whipper, Dobbie, and Lewis pushed him. Arnold's wife, Edna, has apparently had a stroke recently and therefore is not the same woman she used to be. She is a "white-haired woman" with a "worried expression on her face."[82] She is very fearful and tentative, constantly distrusting the world and always reminding her husband not to drive too fast.

In the world of the private home, Arnold and Edna are outsiders who come in for a visit. Each represents a different view of their duty to their fellow human beings. Edna is completely fearful of the world and does not believe that it is an individual's duty to help a person in need, believing instead that "people should mind their own business."[83] She would rather drive past than help Adam out of the ditch. Arnold is just the opposite. He stops and helps Adam in spite of his wife's warning and apprehension. Arnold helps a stranger (Adam) in need. This allows Adam to continue his imaginary search for his father—and his past.

Dr. Dupont

Dr. Dupont is a "big man with white hair and a sad black mustache" whose "voice is always soft, always gentle."[84] Dr. Dupont is a real doctor at the private home. He seems to genuinely care about Adam. He waits for Adam, gives him his medicine, soothes him, and seems genuinely sad when Adam remembers his parents' death. It is Dr. Dupont who unwraps Adam's package for his father and reveals it as Pokey the Pig. He then gives Pokey to Adam in an effort to comfort him.

Adam believes that Dr. Dupont is a kind man and indeed his actions towards Adam seem to be comforting. Adam even tells Brint that Dr. Dupont is kind. However, it is difficult to reconcile the fact that Dr. Dupont assists Brint with this perception of him as a "good guy." Thus, it is probably more accurate to think of Dr. Dupont as Brint with a bit more of a conscience. He still has enough sympathy to feel sorry for Adam. This does not mean that he helps Adam. Dr. Dupont, like Brint, does his job. He sedates Adam to help Brint lead him again and again through the recollection of his parents' murders. Dr. Dupont then feels sad for Adam every time the journey is completed, but this does not lead him to question the morality of his job, help Adam, or quit. He merely tries to comfort Adam after the damage is done.

Mr. Harvester (a.k.a. the Gas Station Attendant).
Mr. Harvester is the maintenance man at the private home. He is a nice, elderly man with white hair and red- and blue-veined face who calls Adam "Skipper." Mr. Harvester still mourns the loss of his son who was killed in World War II at Iwo Jima. According to Adam, Mr. Harvester "mows the lawn and does odd jobs and he is always planning trips somewhere, reading books and maps and travel magazines. But he never goes anywhere."[85]

On Adam's imaginary bike ride Mr. Harvester is the gas station attendant. In this capacity he is both a guide and a harbinger of things to come. It is the gas station attendant who gives Adam a map to help him get to Rutterburg. However, he also tells Adam "it's a terrible world out there" and cautions him that a person "can't tell the good guys from the bad guys anymore."[86]

Mr. Harvester warns Adam not to trust anyone. Adam—and the reader—would be wise to take this advice at this early point in the novel. However, Adam is anxious to leave and afraid that he will be asked about his parents. He fails to heed the warning—as do most readers—and therefore continues to try to trust people even though he does not know who the good guys are.

Arthur Haynes
Arthur Haynes is a white-shirted, sweaty, obese man. In the home, he always stands by the banister watching everyone and scratching himself. On the bike trip, Arthur knows who has taken Adam's bike, but refuses to tell who took it unless he gets a reward.

Arthur is very lonely and the reward he wants seems to be some sort of sexual favor, which would mean that Arthur is a pedophile, preying on children. In this case, the child is seventeen-year-old Adam and Arthur hints that he would appreciate a sexual favor in exchange for his knowledge of the whereabouts of the bicycle.

Arthur represents a form of intimidation that Adam must face. Whereas many of the people who try to stop Adam's journey do so through physical violence, Arthur tries to accomplish this by withholding information in exchange for sexual violence. This frightens Adam so much that all he can do is cry. Luckily, a voice—actually that of Dr. Dupont—breaks in and makes Arthur give Adam the information he desires.

Luke (a.k.a. Lunch Counter Attendant)

Luke is described as a small, thin fellow with a toothpick in his mouth. In the private home, Luke is the switchboard operator—always on the phone in his office at the end of the hallway. At times, Luke also helps serve lunch. When he does, he gives Adam extra portions to fatten him up.

On Adam's imaginary trip, Luke is the counterman at the lunchroom called *Eats*. He serves Adam clam chowder with extra butter. When Whipper, Dobbie, and Lewis pick on him, Adam looks to Luke to step in, but he is on the phone. After Adam stands up to Whipper and gets him to back down, Luke finally steps in to end the harassment. However, he is too late; Adam has already ended it himself. Luke is an example of a person who is capable of helping Adam, but is too busy. When he does finally lend a hand it is too little too late.

Martha Nolan

Martha is Louise's older sister and Adam's aunt. An orphan like her sister, Martha grew up as an Irish Catholic in Blount, New York. She became a nun as a teenager. At the time Adam, her nephew, is fourteen, she lives as a cloistered nun in a convent in Portland, Maine. Martha is Louise's only living relative, her "only link with the world she once knew."[87] Since Martha's convent does not allow any outside visitors, Mr. Grey is willing to take a risk and let Louise call her once a week. These Thursday phone calls make Louise happy. They represent her link to the time of her happiness. However, it is these same Thursday phone calls that further arouse Adam's suspicions and eventually shatter his ignorance of his family's situation.

Silver

Silver is the guard dog at the private home. He is a ferocious German shepherd, sleek and black, that chases the residents of the home. Silver first appears in Adam's imaginary bike trip, although his name is not mentioned, guarding the driveway of a big, deserted, white house. The house is set back from the road and the dog stands growling at the end of the driveway. Adam refers to Silver as a "killer dog" with "eyes like marbles."[88] He feels as though Silver "has been waiting for him his whole life."[89] Even so, Adam musters up his courage and pedals quickly past. The snarling, growling Silver tries to topple his bike, but Adam escapes unharmed. Still, Adam worries that the dog will chase him forever.

Silver then appears, and is named, in Adam's next conversation with Brint. When Adam tells Brint that "the dog is a clue," Brint wonders if he means Silver. Adam is not talking about Silver and instead launches into his story about his father and the dog in the woods.

Finally, Silver reappears by name towards the end of the book at the private home. When Adam's imaginary bike ride concludes and he returns to his room, he must pass Silver in the hall. In this way it is Silver who connects all the separate narratives for the reader for the first time.

When Adam arrives at the private home and sees some of the same people he saw on his bike trip it becomes apparent that the bike trip was imagined. However, it is still unclear where or when Adam's conversations with Brint took place. The reader knows Brint has seen Silver. The fact that Silver exists in Adam's present means that the place where Adam is with Dr. Dupont is the same place Brint resides. This shatters any and all hope for Adam in the final chapter. Thus, Silver represents both a fear that hounds Adam—he hates all dogs—and is also a link between the two presents.

Junior Varney

Junior is a boy of about seventeen, taller and heavier than Adam. Another resident of the private home, Adam says he is always lurking around trying to steal his bike. On the imaginary bike trip, Junior does exactly that. Adam follows him and confronts him. Adam points out that it is never easy to stand up to people, but he knows he must get his bike back. He wrestles Junior for the bike and wins.

Junior Varney is a troublemaker in Adam's world. By stealing the bike, Junior is also trying to intimidate Adam and impede his journey to see his father. Wrestling with Junior Varney is the only physical confrontation Adam has on the journey. Although Adam finds it difficult to fight Junior, he does so because he must see his father—he is determined to remember his past.

Whipper, Dobbie, and Lewis

These are the three troublemakers or wise guys that Adam runs into in the lunchroom. Of the three, he gives a physical description of only one, Whipper. Whipper is about sixteen or seventeen, a bit shorter and heavier than Adam. He has freckles, wide shoulders, and a scar above his beady right eye. The three try to cause trouble for Adam. Whipper attempts to steal the package for Adam's father (it is really Pokey the Pig), taunting Adam and at the same time making fun of his imaginary bike ride. Dobbie and Lewis go along with Whipper and knock Adam off his bike and into a ditch. This then causes a disruption in Adam's journey to see his father and his sessions with Brint.

CHAPTER FIVE

Literary Criticism

In his book on young adult fiction, David Rees told readers that "*I Am the Cheese* is a much better book than *The Chocolate War*. . . . It's a pity that it is not as widely read.["](#)[90] It is also a pity that critics have not paid the sort of attention to *I Am the Cheese* that they did to its predecessor. Indeed, critical literature about *I Am the Cheese* is scarce. Still, that which does exist is quite useful in illuminating the finer points of Cormier's novel.

Realism

One of the first tasks for critics of *I Am the Cheese* was to define what type of young adult fiction it was. An early review of the book applauded Cormier's "knack for making horror out of the ordinary,"[91] and many critics reinforced this view of the book's ordinary and realistic horror. They did so by citing *I Am the Cheese* as an example of realism in young adult fiction.

Realism refers to a style of fiction in which the characters are neither more brave nor more evil than ordinary people, neither superheroes nor villains. Instead, they are everyday people whose actions are plausibly brave, good, or evil. The settings are also ordinary and no more picturesque than everyday life. Essentially, a realistic novel presents a fictional world that seems as though it is the world in which the reader lives. In the words of M. H. Abrams, it gives "the sense that its characters might in fact exist, and that such things might well happen."[92]

Critics concur that Adam is a realistic character. Lance Salway mentions that Adam is a hero who "is an unwilling, uncomprehending and truly innocent victim,"[93] and indeed Adam is in no way extraordinary. A loner, a teenager riddled with fears, insecurities, and stomachaches, Adam is truly average. William J. O'Malley points out that even Adam's courage—or "pluck"—is realistic. He's not a hero in the same way Superman or Tom Swift is, "he's scared. But he's going. He has pluck. . . . Real pluck; coward's pluck."[94]

On the other hand, the events of the novel are not quite as believable as Adam the character. In fact, as critic Perry Nodelman points out, the plot is rather absurd and improbable: a young boy finds out his parents have lied to him about his entire life because his father testified against organized crime. The boy is now at the mercy of an interrogator, and if he tells him everything, he will be killed. This all sounds a bit implausible, as though it would not occur in everyday life.

However, to be an example of realism in fiction, the *plot* of the novel does not need to be realistic. Characters such as Adam can have extraordinary and even absurd adventures, just as long as these events are described—almost reported—matter-of-factly. The way events are presented—the author's writing style—makes the plot seem probable. Critics have applauded Cormier's ability to present the out-of-the-ordinary events of Adam's life realistically, declaring as Rebecca Lukens says, that "Cormier has written skillfully, with plausible happenings and shocking attacks on the reader's sensibilities."[95]

Thus, because of its realistic characters and the way Cormier has written, *I Am the Cheese* is frequently referred to as a realistic young adult fiction novel. Cormier himself suggested this in a 1991 interview when he said, "I like to call myself a realistic writer. I think I probably could summarize it best by saying that I take real people and put them in extraordinary situations."[96]

Problem Novels and New Realism

Although *I Am the Cheese* is frequently referred to as realistic young adult fiction, some critics argue that realism should not be used to describe any fiction. Some assert that the term "realism" has been used to describe too much literature. So much so that it is no longer a useful way of thinking about a text. Still other critics argue there is absolutely no way a fictional work can be truly realistic and at best, one book can only be said to be more realistic than another; for example, *I Am the Cheese* can be said to be *more* realistic than some other young adult novels.

However, critics use literary terms such as "realism" to describe a group of books that are similar in a variety of ways and represent a trend in literature. Quite a few critics saw one such trend in young adult fiction and attempted to clarify that trend. Since they did not care for the term "realistic" that was being applied to the novels, they began to refer to books such as *I Am the Cheese* as either problem novels or examples of New Realism.

Every novel deals with a problem, but some critics call realistic young adult fiction books that deal with complex issues—such as death, drug addiction, and sexual assault—"problem novels." Others, Kenneth Donelson and Alleen Pace Nilsen among them, chose to use the term "New Realism" to describe these same books. For the most part, the two terms are used interchangeably. They describe a specific group of books that, according to Donelson and Nilsen, have the following in common:

1. They are young adult fiction books.

2. They represent an author's honest attempt to depict people in ordinary situations without sentimentalizing or glossing over anything.
3. The protagonists mostly come from lower-class families.
4. The stories are set in harsh, difficult places to live.
5. Authors write realistic dialogue, reflecting the way people talk. They use profanity and ungrammatical construction.
6. They attempt to give readers a realistic picture of life, the good and the bad.

For this reason, readers find that in critical literature all three terms are used to describe *I Am the Cheese*. Depending on the critic, the book is classified as a problem novel, an example of realism in young adult fiction, or an example of New Realism.

Tragedy

Donelson and Nilsen argue that *I Am the Cheese* fits into another category, or genre, of fiction. It resembles a traditional form of literature known as tragedy. This form of literature was originally described by a Greek philosopher named Aristostle. He used concepts such as the tragic hero, a fatal flaw, and catharsis to classify works of literature or drama as tragedy.

Donelson and Nilsen use Aristotle's descriptions as a guideline to argue that tragedies have three essential elements: a tragic hero, an inevitable force that works against the hero, and a struggle and an outcome. These critics argue that *I Am the Cheese* has all three of these factors. Adam is a tragic hero, a character who is better than the average person—more brave, honest, or good. Adam struggles against government corruption and injustice; the outcome is grim.

Donelson and Nilsen also use Aristotle's concept of a fatal flaw—something about the tragic hero that contributes to the unfolding of the tragic events. In *I Am the Cheese*, they assert that if Adam had not been "so bright and inquisitive (which were the characteristics that first brought trouble to his father) and had not found out his family's history, then maybe life could have gone on as before. . . . But at the same time, it is this brightness and persistence that keeps him from surrendering at the end."[97]

One final way to distinguish a tragedy from other forms of literature is the experience of the reader. In a tragedy, the reader is said to feel pity and fear: pity for the defeated protagonist and fear that the same thing could happen in his or her own life. This sort of involvement in the story can lead the reader to experience an emotional release that Aristotle called a catharsis. A catharsis is usually thought of as a purging and purification of emotions, "which has the effect of draining away dangerous human emotions and filling the reader with a sense of exaltation or amazed pride in what the human spirit is called upon to undergo."[98] In other words, the reader of *I Am the Cheese* would close the book with pride about the fact that Adam is still pedaling his bike, still fighting the good fight despite the helpless situation in which he is trapped.

Evil

Unless the reader is rooting for the bad guys, the ending of *I Am the Cheese* is tragic because evil wins. In the book, evil lurks everywhere. Since the book's publication in 1977, Cormier's portrayal of evil has been a favorite topic of discussion among critics.

While Cormier conveys to the reader that "evil surrounds us and will continue to do so,"[99] the evil he portrays is not typical or easily identifiable. Robbie March-Penny asserts that "as the various strands of the story unwind we realize that we the readers, like Adam, do not know who the bad guys are."[100] This can be seen in the character Mr. Grey. No one knows whether or not he is a bad guy. Maia Pank Mertz argues that his very name "grey" suggests that there is no black and white way of defining him. Instead, he represents the gray areas and "embodies the ambiguities of good and evil."[101]

According to Anne Scott MacLeod, it is difficult to define evil in Cormier's work because individuals themselves are not evil and evil itself is not a personality fault that can be explained by psychology or a character's prior experience. MacLeod argues that Cormier presents an evil that comes about only as "a collaborative act between individuals and political systems,"[102] an evil that starts when individuals stop making moral choices for themselves and instead allow a system—governmental or otherwise—to make these choices for them.

For example, readers have no idea what is going on in Brint's mind; his life experiences are not told. They know only that his actions harm Adam. Cormier gives no insight as to why Brint is willing to harm a teenager. He remarked that the only thing known about Brint is that "Adam comes to him completely innocent in his amnesia, and Brint corrupts that. That's what evil is, the destruction of innocence."[103]

However, although readers recognize that Brint harms Adam at the end of the novel, from the tone of Brint's annual report he seems to believe he is merely doing his job for the department. He is part of the system and never questions whether the work he does is morally right or wrong. For Patricia J. Campbell, this is what makes Brint so frightening, that "the worst thing we know about Brint is that he *is* (or *was*) a human being, but he has been so corrupted by his immersion in evil that he can sit year after year across from Adam, calmly herding him through lacerating self-discoveries and feeling not one flicker of pity or mercy."[104]

Nancy Veglahn appreciates Cormier's work precisely because of characters such as Brint. She argues that Cormier is "one of the few writers of realistic young adult fiction who creates genuinely evil characters."[105] According to Veglahn, Cormier's "bad guys" are not merely going through a nasty phase. They are truly evil, and evil truly exists. Therefore, the world will not be a better place if everyone tries to be a better person, just a little bit nicer. Instead, good people will have to fight to overcome the evil in the world. She explains that Cormier's evil characters "present the appearance of harmlessness" and "play roles that are usually associated with helping the young."[106] Brint, for example, seems harmless and even helpful throughout most of a first reading of *I Am the Cheese*. Evil characters then use their power and authority to play on the emotions of their victims and "appear to be indifferent to the suffering they cause."[107] Veglahn suggests that these manipulative adults appear indifferent because they have come to care more about the survival of ideas or systems than individuals.

The System vs. the Individual

While evil comes when people turn their moral choices over to the system, fighting against the system is also a theme of Cormier's work. A reviewer of *I Am the Cheese* proclaimed "Adam's story epitomizes the powerlessness of the individual versus the system."[108] Adam, David, and Louise Farmer are individuals, but because of their situation they've been forced to rely on a government system for protection from the system of organized crime.

In the novel, the individuals do not fare very well. They trust—to varying degrees—the government's system and it fails them miserably. This led Rebecca Lukens to remark that in *I Am the Cheese*, "life is filled with sinister elements, government-related ones at that. There is no hope for the honest citizen in today's society."[109] Similarly, David Rees wrote that "the stand of one or two individuals against the whole apparatus of government is hopeless"[110] in *I Am the*

Cheese. Indeed, it does seem that there is very little hope for any individual up against a system.

Robbie March-Penny contends that in *I Am the Cheese* it does not even really matter which system the individual is up against. Even though organized crime and the government are two very different, independent systems, Cormier shows that they are alike in a very important way—"ultimately the total system is completely ruthless" and will do anything "to maintain its own supremacy."[111]

Anne Scott MacLeod further explains this theme in relation to Mr. Grey. She points out that Mr. Grey's role in the death of Adam's parents is unclear. He was

> supposedly the family's government protector. Might he have been instead their betrayer? Which side did he really work for? As the narrative rolls coldly on, it occurs to the reader that it hardly matters. And this is clearly Cormier's point. The two systems are equally impersonal, and equally dangerous to the human being caught between them. What matters to the organization—*either* organization—is its own survival, not Adam's.[112]

Despair and Hope

The final paragraph of *I Am the Cheese* leaves the reader with very little hope for Adam. Anthony Delmonte has been defeated by the system he attempted to help. His son Paul (now Adam) has become an innocent victim of the same system. Adam is beginning his journey again, a painful journey that he will spend the rest of his life repeating until he either "obliterates," or the current bylaws are changed so that he can be "terminated." The novel offers no alternative.

This disturbing ending led to a debate about the overall message of *I Am the Cheese*. A great deal of the literary criticism about the book focuses around this discussion. Some critics argue that the overall message of the book is one of hopelessness. Lukens suggests that in *I Am the Cheese* "the forces of evil prevail and despair is the winner."[113] While Rees also believes the message is dismal, he adds that "there is no good reason why a teenage novel should not express total despair: the young do not have to be protected in this way."[114]

Some critics agree that the reader feels a sense of despair at book's end, but disagree that the overall message of the work is negative. One such person is Anne Scott MacLeod who admits that Cormier describes "a world of painful harshness" and that the book is "unequivocally downbeat,"[115] but maintains that the book also has a positive message for young adults. She contends this more positive message is frequently overlooked because it is political.

MacLeod reasons that since most young adult books deal with individuals—their personal, psychological, and moral development—the political message, a warning about the danger of ignorance, has been disregarded. This warning—which she claims is the most "insistent" message—is roughly "what you fail to understand about your world can destroy you, either literally or as a human being,"[116] and is an important, and positive, moral for young adults to take away from their reading.

Sylvia Patterson Iskander goes so far as to scold readers who complain about the hopelessness and despair of Cormier's work. She argues that these people are merely angry because the ending of the novel goes against their expectations. Iskander claims this is done purposefully so that readers feel justice has been horribly miscarried and then they are converted to action in their own lives. In other words, upsetting readers with a miscarriage of justice makes them "move beyond the close of the [novel] to a new sense of personal responsibility."[117] According to Iskander, the ultimate, positive message of the book is that "from the defeat of the protagonists who struggle for right in an evil, corrupt and convincingly real world . . . can come the wisdom and understanding of the next generation of individuals who will fight tyranny, who will stand up for their principles, who will be the heroes trying to make the world a better place."[118]

Structure

An early review applauded *I Am the Cheese* for its "highly sophisticated style, and the plotting and literary workmanship."[119] In general, the structure of *I Am the Cheese* has fascinated critics who have responded by attempting to dissect the book and figure out how it works. Both Perry Nodelman and Patricia J. Campbell break the book down into three separate narratives: (1) the first-person narration of a bike ride in the present tense; (2) the discussion between Brint and Adam also in the present tense; (3) Adam's memories that are triggered by the sessions with Brint told in third-person past tense. The book's movement between these three narratives makes up its external structure. This structure, Maia Pank Mertz and many other critics argue, is "integral to the story."[120]

Perry Nodelman suggests that Cormier actually uses this structure to make the reader feel the same emotions that Adam himself does. According to Nodelman, Cormier cleverly structures the book to do a Number—similar to those carried out by Amy Hertz and Adam—on the reader of *I Am the Cheese*. Cormier deceives readers by focusing their attention on the past and confusing them about the present. This, Nodelman says, is accomplished by "providing *one* genuine past, a set of events that happened and are now over, and what appear to be *two* different presents."[121] The reader never guesses the real truth that is right in front of his or her eyes—both the bike ride and the questioning are going on in the same present. If readers figured this out in the first three chapters, the book would not work. However, readers become so intent on figuring out the past, perhaps believing that it will clarify the present, that they put off figuring out Adam's present situation.

Nodelman also argues that by confusing readers and misdirecting their attention, the structure allows Cormier to convince the reader of the truth of three falsehoods: (1) Brint is a doctor; (2) Adam is Adam; and (3) Adam is on a bike trip. The result is that readers have an experience similar to Adam's. Nodelman writes that

> both Adam and those who read about him believe that he is an ordinary member of an ordinary family, and over-prone to foolish suspicions; that Brint is a therapist and that Adam is his mentally disturbed patient; and that Adam is on a bike trip to visit his father in a hospital. Adam's discoveries are more horrifying, and the disorientation that results from them more intense, because Cormier provides readers that same faith in untruths that Adam has, the same discoveries, and the same awesome sense of having trusted too much."[122]

Finally, other critics such as William J. O'Malley, suggest that the three narratives work in additional capacities. He remarked that "the inter-cutting of the plots is masterful: just as the tape is about to uncover another climax, there is the marvelously infuriating cut back to the boy on the bike . . . [it] makes your heart race as if you were pedaling yourself."[123] In other words, jumping back and forth between narratives helps the reader feel the building suspense and frustration among other emotions.

Notes

Introduction

1. Audrey Laski, "No Laughing Matter: Audrey Laski on Fiction for Young Adults," *The Times Educational Supplement*, November 18, 1977, p. 34.

2. Patricia Head, "Robert Cormier and the Postmodernist Possibilities of Young Adult Fiction," *Children's Literature Association Quarterly*, Spring 1996, p. 29.

Chapter 1: The Life of Robert Cormier

3. Robert C. Laserte, "Massachusetts History and Description of Leominster, Massachusetts." http://ci.leominster.ma.us/aboutleo.html.

4. Quoted in *Something About the Author: Reflections of a Small-town Editor*. New York: Delacorte Press, 1991, vol. 45, p. 59.

5. Robert Cormier, *I Have Words to Spend: Reflections of a Small-Town Editor*. New York: Delacorte Press, 1991, pp. 29–30.

6. Quoted in Patricia J. Campbell, *Presenting Robert Cormier*. Boston: Twayne Publishers, 1985, p. 12.

7. Cormier, *I Have Words to Spend*, p. 26.

8. Cormier, *I Have Words to Spend*, p. 26.

9. E-mail from Robert Cormier to author sent November 12, 1999.

10. E-mail from Robert Cormier to author sent November 12, 1999.

11. E-mail from Robert Cormier to author sent November 12, 1999.

12. Cormier, *I Have Words to Spend*, pp. 23–24.

13. Quoted in *Something About the Author*, vol. 45, p. 59.

14. Cormier, *I Have Words to Spend*, p. 27.

15. Geraldine DeLuca and Roni Natov, "Interview with Robert Cormier," *The Lion and the Unicorn: A Critical Journal of Children's Literature*, Spring 1978, p. 109.

16. Quoted in *Something About the Author*, vol. 45, p. 60.

17. Campbell, *Presenting Robert Cormier*, p. 14.

18. Cormier, *I Have Words to Spend*, p. 22.

19. Quoted in *Something About the Author*, vol. 45, p. 60.

20. Quoted in *Something About the Author*, vol. 45, p. 60.

21. E-mail from Robert Cormier to author sent November 12, 1999.

22. Quoted in *Something About the Author*, vol. 45, p. 60.

23. Quoted in *Something About the Author*, vol. 45, p. 60.

24. Paul Janeczko, "In Their Own Words: An Interview with Robert Cormier," *English Journal*, September 1977, p. 10.

25. Campbell, *Presenting Robert Cormier*, p. 16.

26. Janeczko, "In Their Own Words," p. 10.

27. E-mail from Robert Cormier to author sent November 12, 1999.

28. Cormier, *I Have Words to Spend*, p. 200.

29. Quoted in Campbell, *Presenting Robert Cormier*, p. 18.

30. Quoted in Tony Schwartz, "Teen-Agers' Laureate," *Newsweek*, July 16, 1979, p. 88.

31. Quoted in Roger Sutton, "A Conversation with Robert Cormier: 'Kind of a Funny Dichotomy'," *School Library Journal*, June 1991, p. 31.

32. DeLuca and Natov, "An Interview with Robert Cormier," pp. 109–10.

33. Robert Cormier, "The Cormier Novels: The Cheerful Side of Controversy," *Catholic Library World*, July/August, 1978, p. 6.

34. Robert Cormier, *Eight Plus One: Stories by Robert Cormier*. New York: Pantheon Books, 1980, p. vii.

35. *Horn Book Guide*, Spring 1993, p. 66.

36. E-mail from Robert Cormier to author sent November 12, 1999.

37. E-mail from Robert Cormier to author sent November 12, 1999.

38. E-mail from Robert Cormier to author sent November 12, 1999.

Chapter 2: The Impact of the Novel

39. Kenneth L. Donelson and Alleen Pace Nilsen, *Literature for Today's Young Adults*. New York: Harper Collins Publishers, 1989, p. 13.

40. Donna E. Norton, *Through the Eyes of a Child: An Introduction to Children's Literature.* New York: MacMillan Publishing Company, Merrill, 1991, p. 72.

41. Roger Sutton, "The Critical Myth: Realistic YA Novels," *School Library Journal*, November 1982, p. 33.

42. Anne Scott MacLeod, "Robert Cormier and the Adolescent Novel," *Children's Literature in Education*, Summer 1981, p. 74.

43. MacLeod, "Robert Cormier and the Adolescent Novel," p. 75.

44. Quoted in DeLuca and Natov, "An Interview with Robert Cormier," p. 126.

45. Quoted in DeLuca and Natov, "An Interview with Robert Cormier," p. 126.

46. Quoted in DeLuca and Natov, "An Interview with Robert Cormier," p. 122.

47. Quoted in DeLuca and Natov, "An Interview with Robert Cormier," p. 122.

48. Lance Salway, "Death and Destruction," *Times Literary Supplement*, December 2, 1977, p. 1415.

49. Laski, "No Laughing Matter," p. 34.

50. Robert Bell, "*I Am the Cheese*," *The School Librarian*, September 1978, p. 281.

51. Quoted in Laurel Graeber, "PW Interviews: Robert Cormier," *Publishers Weekly*, October 7, 1983, p. 98.

52. Quoted in Betsy Hearne and Marilyn Kaye, eds., *Celebrating Children's Books: Essays on Children's Literature in Honor of Zena Sutherland.* New York: Lothrup, Lee & Shepard Books, 1981, p. 49.

53. Quoted in Hearne and Kaye, eds., *Celebrating Children's Books*, p. 53.

54. MacLeod, "Robert Cormier and the Adolescent Novel," p. 75.

55. MacLeod, "Robert Cormier and the Adolescent Novel," p. 76.

56. Quoted in DeLuca and Natov, "An Interview with Robert Cormier," p. 127.

57. Paul Heins, "*I Am the Cheese*," *Horn Book Magazine*, August 1977, p. 428.

58. Newgate Callendar, "Boy on the Couch," *The New York Times Book Review*, May 1, 1977, p. 26.

59. Salway, *"Death and Destruction,"* p. 1415.

60. Margery Fisher, "Significant Forms," *Growing Point*, April 1978, p. 3286.

61. Callendar, "Boy on the Couch," p. 26.

62. Quoted in Sutton, "A Conversation with Robert Cormier," p. 30.

63. Cormier, "The Cormier Novels," p. 7.

64. Quoted in *Contemporary Authors: New Revision Series*, "Cormier, Robert," vol. 23, p. 91.

65. *The Junior Bookshelf*, "Review," June 1978, p. 151.

66. Salway, "Death and Destruction," p. 1415.

67. Laski, "No Laughing Matter," p. 34.

68. Laski, "No Laughing Matter," p. 34.

Chapter 3: The Plot

69. Perry Nodelman, "Robert Cormier Does a Number," *Children's Literature in Education*, Summer 1983, pp. 95–96.

Chapter 4: The Cast of Characters

70. Quoted in DeLuca and Natov, "An Interview with Robert Cormier," p. 128.

71. Quoted in Alleen Pace Nilsen, "The Poetry of Naming in Young Adult Books," *The ALAN Review*, Spring 1980, p. 4.

72. Robert Cormier, *I Am the Cheese*. New York: Dell Laurel-Leaf Books, 1991, p. 12.

73. Cormier, *I Am the Cheese*, p. 134.

74. E-mail from Robert Cormier to author on November 12, 1999.

75. Cormier, *I Am the Cheese*, p. 57.

76. Cormier, *I Am the Cheese*, p. 117.

77. Cormier, *I Am the Cheese,* p. 118.

78. Cormier, *I Am the Cheese,* p. 117.

79. Nilsen, "The Poetry of Naming in Young Adult Books," p. 4.

80. Cormier, *I Am the Cheese,* p. 56.

81. Cormier, *I Am the Cheese,* p. 110.

82. Cormier, *I Am the Cheese,* p. 111.

83. Cormier, *I Am the Cheese,* p. 111.

84. Cormier, *I Am the Cheese,* p. 212.

85. Cormier, *I Am the Cheese,* p. 212.

86. Cormier, *I Am the Cheese,* p. 24.

87. Cormier, *I Am the Cheese,* p. 159.

88. Cormier, *I Am the Cheese,* p. 36.

89. Cormier, *I Am the Cheese,* p. 36.

Chapter 5: Literary Criticism

90. David Rees, *The Marble in the Water: Essays on Contemporary Writers of Fiction for Children and Young Adults.* Boston: The Horn Book Company, Inc., 1980, p. 159.

91. Callendar, "Boy on the Couch," p. 26.

92. M. H. Abrams, *A Glossary of Literary Terms.* Fort Worth, TX: Harcourt Brace Jovanovich College Publishers, 1993, p. 174.

93. Salway, "Death and Destruction," p. 1415.

94. William J. O'Malley, "A Review of *I Am the Cheese,*" *Media & Methods,* May/June 1978, p. 26.

95. Quoted in Joseph Milner, ed., *Webs and Wardrobes: Humanist and Religious World Views in Children's Literature.* Lanham, MD: University Press of America, 1987, p. 11.

96. Quoted in Sutton, "A Conversation with Robert Cormier: 'Kind of a Funny Dichotomy,'" p. 28.

97. Donelson and Nilsen, *Literature for Today's Young Adults,* p. 88.

98. Donelson and Nilsen, *Literature for Today's Young Adults,* p. 88.

99. Sylvia Patterson Iskander, "Readers, Realism, and Robert Cormier," *Children's Literature: Annual of the Modern Language Association Division on Children's Literature and the Children's Literature Association*, 1987, p. 12.

100. Robbie March-Penny, "From Hardback to Paperback: *The Chocolate War*, by Robert Cormier," *Children's Literature in Education*, Summer 1978, pp. 80–81.

101. Maia Pank Mertz, "Enhancing Literary Understandings Through Young Adult Fiction," *Publishing Research Quarterly*, Spring 1992, p. 32.

102. MacLeod, "Robert Cormier and the Adolescent Novel," p. 79.

103. Campbell, *Presenting Robert Cormier*, p. 64.

104. Campbell, *Presenting Robert Cormier*, p. 62.

105. Nancy Veglahn, "The Bland Face of Evil in the Novels of Robert Cormier," *The Lion and the Unicorn: A Critical Journal of Children's Literature*, June 1988, p. 12.

106. Veglahn, "The Bland Face of Evil in the Novels of Robert Cormier," p. 12.

107. Veglahn, "The Bland Face of Evil in the Novels of Robert Cormier," p. 13.

108. *Booklist*, "Books for Young Adults," April 1, 1977, p. 1156.

109. Quoted in Milner, ed., *Webs and Wardrobes*, p. 11.

110. Rees, *The Marble in the Water*, p. 158.

111. March-Penny, "From Hardback to Paperback," pp. 80–81.

112. MacLeod, "Robert Cormier and the Adolescent Novel," pp. 76–77.

113. Quoted in Milner, ed., *Webs and Wardrobes*, p. 11.

114. Rees, *The Marble in the Water*, p. 158.

115. MacLeod, "Robert Cormier and the Adolescent Novel," p. 74.

116. MacLeod, "Robert Cormier and the Adolescent Novel," p. 80.

117. Iskander, "Readers, Realism, and Robert Cormier," p.17.

118. Iskander, "Readers, Realism, and Robert Cormier," p.17.

119. Callendar, "Boy on the Couch," p. 26.

120. Mertz, "Enhancing Literary Understandings Through Young Adult Fiction," p. 30.

121. Nodelman, "Robert Cormier Does a Number," pp. 95–96.

122. Nodelman, "Robert Cormier Does a Number," p. 100.

123. O'Malley, "A Review of *I Am the Cheese*," p. 26.

For Further Exploration

Below are some suggestions for themes or essays that could be written about *I Am the Cheese*.

1. Keep a reading journal and read *I Am the Cheese* twice. At the end of each chapter write down what happened, what you know, and any questions you might have. Compare and contrast the two readings. *See also*: Phyllis Bixler, "*I Am the Cheese* and Reader-Response Criticism in the Adolescent Literature Classroom," *Children's Literature Quarterly*, Spring 1985; Nodelman, "Robert Cormier Does a Number."

2. In *I Am the Cheese*, Anthony Delmonte (David Farmer) tries to be a good citizen and help the government fight organized crime. As a result, eventually he and his wife are murdered and their child, Paul/Adam, is left in danger of being killed. Why do Anthony and Adam—who could be thought of as the "good guys"—fail in their attempts to fight the evil of organized crime and government corruption? *See also:* March-Penny, "From Hardback to Paperback"; MacLeod, "Robert Cormier and the Adolescent Novel"; Donelson and Nilsen, *Literature for Today's Young Adults*.

3. In a 1981 essay, Robert Cormier described the type of fear he was trying to convey to readers of *I Am the Cheese*: "The phone clicks. I think twenty [now more than forty] years ago we'd have thought, 'Well, there's something wrong with the line.' Today, there's a click and you wonder. And if there's no click, you think, well, they're so sophisticated today, they can even listen without a click. So I wanted to portray [this] kind of fear that is in our lives today." Does Cormier successfully convey this fear? To help answer the question, list Adam's fears and find instances in the book where he is fearful. *See also:* Cormier, "Forever Pedaling on the Road to Realism."

4. Over the course of the book Adam feels many different emotions such as fear, depression, and confusion. Examine the book's three different narratives—(1) The tapes of Adam talking to Brint; (2) Adam remembering the past; and (3) the bike ride. How do these

three narratives and the switching between them make the reader feel some of the same emotions Adam feels? *See also:* Nodelman, "Robert Cormier Does a Number."

5. In what ways does Cormier's writing style—the words he chooses, his sentence length, the rhythm of these sentences—work to make the reader feel some of the same emotions that Adam does? *See also:* Mertz, "Enhancing Literary Understandings Through Young Adult Fiction."

6. The children's song "The Farmer in the Dell" appears throughout *I Am the Cheese*. Adam sings different verses at various times. Also, the Delmonte family's witness protection name is Farmer, and the book's title is taken from the song. How does Cormier use the song in the book? What might it symbolize? *See also:* Rebecca Luken's essay in Milner, ed., *Webs and Wardrobes*, pp. 7–13; Pace Nilsen, "The Poetry of Naming in Young Adult Books."

7. Anthony Delmonte and his son stand up to a variety of systems throughout the novel. Anthony tries to stand up to organized crime. Paul/Adam fights against the government. Given their fates, what is Cormier trying to convey about the individual who stands up to the system? *See also:* March-Penny, "From Hardback to Paperback"; MacLeod, "Robert Cormier and the Adolescent Novel."

8. Discuss Cormier's portrayal of evil. Start by answering the following questions: Which characters are evil and why? What does this suggest about what Cormier is trying to show about the nature of evil in the novel? *See also:* Veglahn, "The Bland Face of Evil in the Novels of Robert Cormier"; MacLeod, "Robert Cormier and the Adolescent Novel."

9. According to Kenneth Donelson and Alleen Pace Nilsen, tragedies have three elements: a tragic hero; an inevitable force that works against the hero; and a struggle leading to an outcome. The noble hero also frequently has a fatal flaw—something about the character that contributes to the unfolding of the tragic events. Does *I Am the Cheese* contain all these elements? Could it be called a tragedy, or is it just sad? *See also:* Sutton, "The Critical Myth"; Donelson and Nilsen, *Literature for Today's Young Adults.*

10. Throughout the novel Adam tells the reader that he is frightened; however, he does things that might be considered brave or courageous. Describe at least three instances in the book where Adam is brave. How does he feel at the time? What might Cormier be trying to suggest about the nature of bravery and courage? *See also:* O'Malley, "A Review of *I Am the Cheese*."

Appendix of Criticism

Reviews

Adam's "Secret" Explodes Like an H-Bomb

The author of *The Chocolate War* has written another novel which scores a direct hit on the nerves. It is, however, entirely different. A thriller packed with menace and superbly constructed. Adam Farmer is a 14-year-old boy fleeing from home in a Massachusetts town by bicycle to find his father in Rutterburg, Vermont. Adam's first-person narration is interspersed by passages of questions and answers between him and a psychiatrist. As the boy's journey continues, he's beset by young hoods trying to steal the precious package he's carrying. Gradually, we learn that Adam has been disturbed by puzzling happenings at home and by the periodic appearances of a cold, bossy stranger. Slowly, he discovers that his family has been hiding out, under new identities, in fear of their lives. The secret, revealed at the end, explodes like an H-bomb.

Publishers Weekly, March 7, 1977. Reprinted with permission.

Suspense and Powerlessness

Teenaged Adam Farmer's discovery of two conflicting birth certificates and his subsequent eavesdropping around the house cause Adam to wonder about himself, his parents, and their everyday lives. Confronting his father, he learns that Mr. Farmer's testimony before a Senate committee years earlier had placed the family in such danger that the government relocated them with new identities. Ever since, their lives have been tightly controlled by a special government agency. Past and present events, shaded by a sense of unreality, commingle in the complex but tightly structured plot, which slowly reveals Adam's current condition through three smoothly integrated alternating narratives—one of which involves his sessions with a therapist/interrogator. The suspense builds relentlessly to an ending that, although shocking, is entirely plausible. The characterizations have substance, and the theme, advanced with more subtlety here than in *The Chocolate War* (Pantheon, 1974), is no less chilling in impact and implication: Adam's story epitomizes the powerlessness of the individual versus the system.

"Books for Young Adults," *Booklist*, April 1, 1977. Reprinted with permission.

85

Too Difficult for Teen Readers?

Cormier has written a novel of psychological suspense. He is a fine technician and this is an absorbing, even a brilliant job. The book is assembled in mosaic fashion: a tiny chip here, a chip there, and suddenly the outline of a face dimly begins to take shape. Everything is related to something else; everything builds and builds to a fearsome climax. At the end the boy discovers that he is indeed the cheese—the bait around which the rats gather. Little can he do about it, except react the way God and Freud have provided. The ending is grim indeed.

It is not that *I Am the Cheese* is in any way sensational, sadistic or anything like that. Cormier merely has the knack of making horror out of the ordinary, as the masters of suspense writing know how to do. The story moves along quietly enough. The bicycling adventures of the boy are the kind of adventures anybody today could experience. Where the tension enters is in the mind of the boy, who (as it turns out) is faced with a situation with which no child should have to cope.

The book is written in a highly sophisticated style, and the plotting and literary workmanship will delight the connoisseur. But, one wonders, will the style and, indeed, some of the actual content be above the heads of most teen-agers? It may be, however, that kids are more sophisticated today and that nothing much comes as a surprise to them.

Excerpt from Newgate Callendar, "Boy on the Couch,"
New York Times Book Review, May 1, 1977.
© 1977 by The New York Times
Company. Reprinted with permission.

I Am the Cheese Could Harm Disturbed Youth

So few concessions are now made to the adolescent reader that I keep wondering why novels should be specially written for such readers at all: only the fact that the central characters are in their teens differentiate narratives from straight adult novels, and there seems no reason to suppose that adolescents are interested only in their own age group.

Until recently one mark of the novel for young adults that distinguished it from some adult novels was that the narrative mode was straightforward. Alan Garner was probably the pioneer in breaking this barrier: now *I Am the Cheese*, as if it were a *nouvelle vague* text, alternates a first-person present tense account of an alarming cycle ride across New England with a series of tape-recorded interviews between a boy, whom one may assume is the same as the cyclist, and someone who may be a psychiatrist: sometimes the boy's memories in the third person interrupt this colloquy.

Through this complex, and indeed irritating, pattern of narration, a grim story of fear, repression and betrayal establishes itself: the ending, in which one is almost simultaneously confronted with the extent of the boy's insanity and the deadly truth at its root, is entirely bleak, another way in which this novel makes no concessions to the tender sensibilities. What worries me about this book, which admittedly grips intensely once one has come to terms with its manner, is that it could possibly do real harm to a disturbed adolescent, since it communicates all too effectively the paranoid fear that a psychiatric questioner may be an enemy—and then shows that it is true.

> Excerpted from "Audrey Laski, "No Laughing Matter,"
> *The Times Educational Supplement*, November 18, 1977. © Times Supplements limited. Reprinted with permission.

I Am the Cheese Makes Other Teen Novels Look Insignificant

For [*I Am the Cheese*] Robert Cormier has returned to the theme which dominated his outstanding earlier book, *The Chocolate War:* that of innocence and morality destroyed by the ruthless ambition of the masters of a corrupt society. In *The Chocolate War*, this society was the private school, and the victim a boy who alone stood out against corruption. Now, in *I Am the Cheese*, Robert Cormier has extended this dark theme. The hero is an unwilling, uncomprehending and truly innocent victim of a greater, more hideous conspiracy; the corrupt society is our own, and the innocent victim must be completely destroyed in order to sustain it.

At first sight, the narrative construction of the novel seems difficult and pretentious . . . As the novel nears its end, the point and meaning of the book's construction become plain, and the narrative strands combine in a climax of depressing violence and a conclusion of almost intolerable despair . . . Robert Cormier does not hesitate to challenge and disturb his readers and, although *I Am the Cheese* is no book for the emotionally squeamish, it deserves to be widely read. Beside it, most books for the young seem as insubstantial as candyfloss.

> Excerpted from Lance Salway, "Death and Destruction,"
> *The Times Literary Supplement*, December 2, 1977. Reprinted with permission.

Literary Criticism

Adam: A Loveable, Cowardly Hero

What's more, from the first page, the book is pitted with question marks—why is the boy's father in the hospital? why are the dates on the tapes deleted? what possible relation have the tape-chapters to the bicycling-chapters? why does the boy have two birth certificates?—and a question mark is an inverted hook.

Two plots run parallel, converge, throw clue-hooks into one another. They build, become impending, until you know "it" is coming. And yet, right up to the end, you find yourself saying, "What's going *on*???" Then the final chapter takes the whole thing, twists it round, shakes it up, and punches you right in the solar plexus. To put it in no way facetiously, this novel is like *I Never Promised You a Rose Garden* written in collaboration by Ian Fleming and Franz Kafka.

The intercutting of the plots is masterful: just as the tape is about to uncover another climax, there is the marvelously infuriating cut back to the boy on the bike. But it is not just the manipulative plotting that makes your heart race as if you were pedaling yourself. It is the fact that, right from the start, young Adam Farmer has hold of your heart.

You *care* about a kid who tells you, right off, as he's pedaling along, "I pass by a house with a white picket fence and I spot a little kid who's standing on the sidewalk and he watches me go by and I wave to him because he looks lonesome and he waves back." He is claustrophobic, even on baseball fields; he can't stand rooms without windows, even restrooms; mysteriously, he has dumped some kind of pills out just before beginning his frightening little odyssey in search of his father; he is scared. But he's going. He has pluck. Not Tom Swift pluck. Real pluck; coward's pluck.

Excerpted from William J. O'Malley, *Media & Methods*, May/June 1978. Reprinted with permission.

I Am the Cheese Is a Tragedy

Robert Cormier's books come closer to being tragedies. In traditional literary criticism, tragedies have three distinct elements. First there is a noble character who, no matter what happens, maintains the qualities that the society considers praiseworthy; second, there is an inevitable force that works against the character; and, third, there is a struggle and an outcome. In Cormier's *I Am the Cheese*, the boy being interrogated throughout the book is the tragic hero. The inevitable force is corruption and government duplicity. And the outcome—in which the best that the boy can hope for is to live his life in a drugged and incoherent state—is indeed a tragedy. Yet the reader is left with some satisfaction and pride because there is a resiliency in the boy that keeps him, even when he is drugged, from totally surrendering to his highly skilled interrogators.

Another tradition sometimes considered essential in tragedy holds that the hero—worthy and admirable as he or she may be—has nevertheless contributed to the unfolding of the terrible events through some tragic flaw of character. With Cormier's book, the reader has the nagging feeling that maybe if the boy had not been so bright and inquisitive (which were the characteristics that first brought trouble to his father) and had not found out his family's history, then maybe life could have gone on as before and Mr. Grey wouldn't have bothered with him. But at the same time, it is this brightness and persistence that keeps him from surrendering at the end.

The reader of a tragedy is usually filled with pity and fear—pity for the hero and fear for oneself that the same thing might happen. The intensity of this involvement causes the reader to undergo an emotional release as the outcome of the story unfolds. This release is known as catharsis, which has the effect of draining away dangerous human emotions and filling the reader with a sense of exaltation or amazed pride in what the human spirit is called upon to undergo.

Kenneth Donelson and Alleen Pace Nilsen,
Literature for Today's Young Adults. New York:
Harper Collins Publishers, 1989.

I Am the Cheese Is a Political Novel That Warns Readers to Be Aware

Robert Cormier is a conspicuous oddity in his chosen field. Writing for the adolescent reader, he has departed from standard models and broken some of the most fundamental taboos of that vocation. Each of his hard-edged novels for the young goes considerably beyond the standard limits of "contemporary realism" to describe a world of painful harshness, where choices are few and consequences desperate. Moreover, his novels are unequivocally downbeat: all three violate the unwritten rule that fiction for the young, however sternly realistic the narrative material, must offer some portion of hope, must end at least with some affirmative message. Affirmation is hard to find in Cormier's work, and conventional hopefulness is quite irrelevant to it.

But while these sharp breaks with accepted practice have been much noted by reviewers, and have furnished Cormier's reputation for bleakness, curiously little notice has been taken of another, and, to my mind, equally interesting departure from the norm in his novels. Quite aside from his attitudes and conclusions, Cormier is a maverick in the field of adolescent literature because he is writing what are, at bottom, political novels. . . . A consistent feature of almost the whole body of adolescent literature is its isolation from the political and societal, its nearly total preoccupation with personality. The typical adolescent novel is wrapped tightly around the individual and the personal: questions of psychological development and personal morality dominate the genre. . . .

Cormier, on the other hand, is far more interested in the systems by which a society operates than he is in individuals. His novels center on the interplay between individuals and their context, between the needs and demands of the system and the rights of individuals—in other words, on the political context in which his characters, like all of us, must live. He is, obviously, concerned with moral questions, but the morality involved is of a wholly different order from the purely personal moral concerns of most teen novels. . . .

In his second novel, *I Am the Cheese*, Cormier dispenses with metaphor. This stark tale comments directly on the real world of government, organized crime, large-scale bureaucracy, the apparatus of control, secrecy, betrayal, and all the commonplaces of contemporary political life. . . . The optimistic reader will find it hard to locate an exit as the story moves to a conclusion. Adam is doomed, as his parents were; he will be "obliterated" one way or another because he is a threat to one or possibly both of the systems with which his life is entangled. There is certainly some ambiguity about the role played in this tragedy by Mr. Grey, supposedly the family's government protector. Might he have been instead their betrayer? Which side did he really work for? As the narrative rolls coldly on, it occurs to the reader that it hardly matters. And this is clearly Cormier's point. The two systems are equally impersonal, and equally dangerous to the human being caught between them. What matters to the organization—x*either* organization—is its own survival, not Adam's. . . .

[Cormier] writes of things few books for the young acknowledge at all. He has evoked a political world in which evil is neither an individual phenomenon nor a personality fault explainable by individual psychology, but a collaborative act between individuals and political systems which begins when the individual gives over to the system the moral responsibility that is part of being human. He suggests that innocence can be a moral defect, that evil is . . . banal, and, above all, that political bureaucracies are often—perhaps always—a potential danger to individual freedom because they are fundamentally committed to their own perpetuation, which is always threatened by individual dissent.

These are aspects of contemporary reality not often set out in literature for the young, as the reactions of many reviewers attest. Yet the young are not immune to political reality. Far from it, they are its chief inheritors. Though it may be true—it undoubtedly is true—that adolescents are primarily interested in themselves, it does not follow that adults who write for the adolescent readers must share this narrow preoccupation. All of us . . . live in a political as well as a personal world. We are not safer for ignoring it.

Surely, if message there is in Cormier's work, this is the most insistent. I cannot discover that he wants to tell his readers that by recognizing their dangers they can escape them, and I do not think his books can be reduced to a positive statement about the protective virtue of political understanding. "Know your world and you will be safe," is far too bald and optimistic. Put negatively, the proposition may come a little closer: "what you fail to understand about your world can destroy you, either literally or as a human being." Certainly these novels suggest that no one will escape who does not know where the threat lies, how the annihilating process works.

Excerpted from Anne Scott MacLeod,
"Robert Cormier and the Adolescent Novel,"
Children's Literature in Education, Summer 1981.
Reprinted with permission.

New Realism Is Safe and Easy Reading for Teens

With the advent of the problem novel, we were told that times have changed. Until very recently, simple romances were "out" in YA [young adult] realism, replaced by novels about various concerns: drug abuse, premarital sex, and so on. Instead of a character being the focus of the novel, a condition became the subject of examination. With individual books often described as "tough," "honest," and "hard-hitting," the genre became known as the "New Realism." Kenneth Donelson and Alleen Nilsen claim that not only had there been a shift in subject matter in the contemporary realistic novel for young adults, but there had been a shift in fictional mode as well: from the romantic to ironic, and some-times tragic. . . .

Those critics who claim that the New Realism is characterized by a tragic or ironic mode engage in a critical myth-making. Though they may speak to such problems as runaways and prostitution, problem novels are usually about *solutions* to those problems, and the integra-tion of the wayward (or waylaid) protagonist into a responsible, adult society. . . . Taking these books too seriously is not a harmless endeavor; it deludes us into thinking that we are giving young adults truly sub-stantial literature, rather than simply entertaining them. . . .

"What about Robert Cormier?" is a question that must be raised here. Cormier has, to my mind, unreasonably become a symbol for all that is good and bad in adolescent literature. His books are certainly not typical of the New Realism, for two reasons. They have unhappy endings and, as Anne Scott MacLeod has noted, his books do not concern "the individual and the personal," do not concern them-selves for the most part with "psychological development and per-sonal morality," a major preoccupation of the typical realistic novel for teens. . . .

Cormier's three novels all tell compellingly of a universe where the good guys lose. But under the grim, no-win surface lies a very conventional, respectable morality: wrong may triumph over right, but the reader is certainly shown which is which.

When adolescent novels do trade in tragedy, they do so in a very safe way, encouraging readers to identify with an innocent protagonist. All of Cormier's protagonists are virtuous and brave and all of them . . . are trying to do the right thing. They are not victims of their own mistakes or tragic flaws so much as they are victims of an evil beyond their control. . . . Even the most grim, most tragic novels for teenagers leave readers unchallenged and inviolate. They arouse passions of indignation at the evil actions of others, yet do not make the reader confront himself as anything less, or more, than innocent. *Things can go wrong*, these tragic novels say, *but it's not your fault.*

Excerpted from Roger Sutton, "The Critical Myth: Realistic YA Novels," *School Library Journal*, November 1982. Copyright © 1982 by Roger Sutton. Reproduced by permission of the author.

Cormier Deliberately Dashes Readers' Hopes to Encourage Them to Fight Injustice

The reader—parent, schoolboard member, or young adult—who rejects a Cormier novel as totally without hope has failed to recognize its positive elements because these are presented ironically and indirectly. The successful reader must recognize the various levels of reality present in these novels and extrapolate beyond the novel's close to see an extended moral development. . . .

Cormier deliberately violates our optimistic expectations in a strategy designed to convert the reader from a passive to an active role. . . .

In *I Am the Cheese* the individual's stand against evil raises. . . problems. A conscientious newspaperman, Mr. Delmonte, uncovering some corruption in government and believing in civic duty, testifies as a witness. The Department of Re-Identification relocates his family and gives them a new identity as "the Farmers," an ironically all-American name. At the novel's close this family is destroyed—the parents killed and fourteen-year-old Adam Farmer driven to amnesia, his only protection from "termination." Such pessimism conflicts with our social expectations, our myths of participatory democracy, of triumphant patriotism and civic allegiance. The defeat of these myths also defies our literary expectations, and we again feel shocked by Cormier's rejection of the conventions that we adhere to as "real."

But Cormier also incorporates positive materials that show his commitment to democratic values and that give grounds for hope. Mr. Farmer is a warm, concerned father, respected and loved by his son; he is what we expect a model citizen to be. Mrs. Farmer—a stereotypical "good wife"—does not criticize her husband's attempt to do the right thing, although his action vastly changes their lives and leaves her sad and disoriented. Remaining in seclusion much of the time, she tries desperately to maintain the unity of the family by refusing to obey the rules about what items they can keep from their former life or where they can speak without fear of being overheard. As complex and isolated as her life becomes, she remains clear-sighted about their fragile safety and says that the corruption they opposed is "like an evil growth: cut off one part, but who knows about the other parts?"

Cormier seeks to touch deep within his sensitive youthful audience their sense of right and wrong, of fair play, while he refuses to accept the literary and social stereotypes in which these values are so often delivered to the young. The reader's need for reaction depends upon his own ability to feel rage at the miscarriage of justice. . . .

For the reader, unlike the characters, has a second chance. From the defeat of the protagonists who struggle for right in an evil, corrupt, and convincingly real world, where no law of poetic justice prevails, can come the wisdom and understanding of the next generation of individuals who will fight tyranny, who will stand up for their principles, who will be the heroes trying to make the world a better place. . . .

Cormier makes his readers think long after they have closed his novels because he chooses not to follow the literary norm of the happy ending. The climactic structure of his novels with their shocking, unhappy, but quite realistic endings reinforces not the temporary defeats or a bleak pessimism, but rather a longing for justice. His books "argue" for moral responsibility far more effectively than sermonizing or stereotypical formulas of virtue automatically triumphant.

Excerpted from Sylvia Patterson Iskander, "Readers, Realism, and Robert Cormier," *Children's Literature: Annual of the Modern Language Association Division on Children's Literature and the Children's Literature Association*, 1987. Reprinted by permission of Yale University Press.

I Am the Cheese Sends a Message of Total Despair

With the complexity of three interwoven levels, Cormier weaves the story of a boy's psychological search for his father with his search into his memories of the past. The novel revolves and circles in Adam's continuous and frustrating struggle to remember, mingled with a fear of remembering. His search for his dead father cannot end; the novel opens and closes with the same paragraph: "I am riding the bicycle and I am on Route 31 . . . on my way to Rutterburg, Vermont . . . the wind like a snake slithering up my sleeves. . . . But I keep pedaling, I keep pedaling." The circular movement of the novel is like "The Farmer in the Dell," the child's continuous and circular game. Throughout the story, Adam, his father, and his mother sing the song, calling it the Farmer family's own song. The last verse is not sung until the final pages when psychologically damaged Adam, orphaned by the violent gangland murder of both his father and his mother, sings the last lines: "The cheese stands alone . . . I am the cheese." . . .

The enigma of the novel is, how much does Adam Farmer, once Paul Delmonte, know about his past, and more importantly, who needs to find out—Adam or the government? . . . As the story moves back and forth between Adam's bicycle ride through his fantasy and his dialogue with the psychiatrist, we are exposed to the actual events of his life in the present. At the novel's end we discover that Adam is not being psychologically healed after all. The interrogation which seems at times humane and therapeutic is merely politically expedient.

The reader's puzzlement carries the novel along; our fears are never allayed. Adam Farmer/Paul Delmonte will never be able to live free of the annual interrogation, or to move outside the sanitarium walls. The disturbed adolescent who loves Amy Hertz and wants to love her forever is the same dependent child who clutches his stuffed animal, Poley (sic) the Pig. The government is vigilant; should Adam remember all and so be healed, he becomes dangerous. No matter how healthy he might become, Adam will never be able to untangle himself from the maze of regulation and red tape. In his fantasy Adam continues his search for his father and keeps pedaling, keeps pedaling. In reality, he is only a series of digits in a government file.

The effect upon the reader is not merely fear, but often sheer terror . . . of the endlessly connected underworld and of uncontrollable impulses to speak the forbidden or to discover what must be left undiscovered. Again, Cormier has written skillfully, with plausible happenings and shocking attacks on the reader's sensibilities. The effect, once again, is that life is filled with sinister elements, government-related ones at that. There is no hope for the honest citizen in today's society. The forces of evil prevail and despair is the winner.

Excerpted from Rebecca Lukens, "From Salinger to Cormier: Disillusionment to Despair in Thirty Years," in Joseph O'Beirne and Lucy Floyd Morcock Milner, eds., *Webs and Wardrobes: Humanist and Religious World Views in Children's Literature.* Lanham, MD: University Press of America, 1987.

Brint, Mr. Grey, and Cormier's Other Genuinely Evil Characters

Robert Cormier is one of the few writers of realistic fiction for young adults who creates genuinely evil characters. Unlike fantasy and science fiction books, which abound with embodiments of cosmic malevolence, realistic novels seem to shy away from villains. Even school bullies that often provide conflict in modern YA [Young Adult] fiction are made to seem relatively tame, as if they were just going through a nasty phase. There are killers and kidnappers in the mysteries, of course, but these are usually flat characters, never developed enough to take on real stature, always defeated in the end.

Perhaps writers of realistic novels for young readers want to avoid creating the stereotypical black-hatted "bad guy" of movies and TV, or perhaps they have been influenced by modern notions of the little bit of good in everyone and of moral relativity. Flannery O'Connor said that she was "speaking to an audience which does not believe in evil," and that may well be true of most authors of YA novels as well.

It is not true of Robert Cormier. There is no moral blandness in his books, no picture of a world in which all will be well if everyone just tries a little harder. "I've come to realize that Saturday matinees have nothing to do with real life," says Cormier, "that innocence doesn't provide immunity from evil, that the mugger lurking in the doorway assaults both the just and unjust." Readers hoping for the triumph of justice and goodness in Cormier's work are likely to be disappointed.

Yet his evil characters do present the appearance of harmlessness, or even benevolence. . . They play roles that are usually associated with helping the young: parent, teacher, counselor, physician, government official, friend. Each one is able to seem innocuous or attractive when it suits his purposes; each one masquerades as something he is not in order to manipulate the protagonist.

"The evil that is easy to recognize and label is the kind that is easy to combat—but the evil that appears with a bland face isn't," said Cormier in an interview with Merri Rosenberg. This habit of dressing moral monsters in the disguise of kindly helpers has helped to make Robert Cormier the most controversial of all the current authors of books for teenagers. His evil characters not only have faces but also use the authority and power they have to destroy the young. They are adversaries who cannot lose because the contest is unequal, villains who inevitably prevail.

Excerpted from Nancy Veglahn, "The Bland Face of Evil in the Novels of Robert Cormier," *The Lion and the Unicorn* 12:1 (1988), pp. 12–13. © *The Johns Hopkins University Press. Reprinted with permission,* June 1988.

Cormier: Structure and Style

I Am the Cheese is consistently one of the most difficult novels for my college students, yet also one of their favorite works for analysis.

Cormier's novel is particularly appropriate for dealing with two concepts that inexperienced readers seem to find particularly elusive: *style* and *structure*. . . . In her chapter on *I Am the Cheese*, [Patricia J.] Campbell states that the "triple strands that are braided together to make the story, the three alternating levels on which the narrative progresses, are an intricate but internally consistent device." According to Campbell, these are the three levels of narrative:

> The bike ride is told in first-person present tense. The tapes, as dialogue, have neither person nor tense (but we assume they are happening in the present), and the revelation of Adam's past that grows out of these tapes proceeds chronologically and is in third-person past tense.

Structurally, then, there are three levels of the story, and three points of view. As Campbell notes, this is extremely confusing when the novel is read for the first time. Only in subsequent readings does it become possible to see the relationships that exist among the various levels. . . .

Although the internal structure of the novel is complex, the external structure—the juxtaposition of the "tapes" with the bike journey and the past—provides a means to start discussions of structure. After reading the first two chapters, readers can begin to understand how the writer is using the different levels and points of view to move the story forward. What emerges, then, is a structure or form that is integral to the story. In effect, form and content merge. The way the story is told is essential to the content of the story. A clear example of how the structure relates to the story is that the opening lines of the novel are repeated at the end. The story is cyclical. Like Adam's interrogations, it begins anew.

If structure is the overall form of the story, the design that the author has used, *style* constitutes the manner of expression that the writer has chosen to tell the story. Young readers seem to understand the term best when it is simply described as *how* the author tells the story. Consistently, Cormier's style captures the pace and intensity of the events in the story.

Excerpted from Maia Pank Mertz,
"Enhancing Literary Understandings Through
Young Adult Fiction," *Publishing Research Quarterly*, Spring 1992.
Copyright © 1992 by Transaction Publishers; all rights reserved.
Reprinted by permission of Transaction Publishers.

Cormier and the "Compromise of Survival"

Valuable . . . is the work of writers such as Robert Cormier . . . who are . . . concerned with the essential sadness of the inevitable passing from innocence to experience—the compromise of survival. Teenagers need to be able to say, "yes: so that's how you cope with it" and novels that *show them how* are likely to be more helpful to the imaginative and emotional growth of the young people than those that take issues—drugs, venereal disease, or whatever—as starting points. . . .

There is little obvious compromise in *I Am the Cheese*, for political power and corruption are . . . illustrated . . . by the power of the government itself, and Cormier's message here is much more bleak: that the stand of one or two individuals against the whole apparatus of government is hopeless. Adam, the central character, is someone we might find in many novels for young adults, a teenager who is struggling to find—on many levels—who he is and what his place in the world should be. We see his first meaningful love affair and we explore the complexities of his feelings for his parents; but what makes Adam's situation so different from that of the hero in almost all teenage fiction is that the reader knows, at the end of the book, that he is going to die; either he will be "terminated" as his parents were, or the treatment will "obliterate" him. Complaints by critics that the hopelessness of *I Am the Cheese* is inappropriate to a story for young people are not justifiable in my opinion; there is no good reason why a teenage novel should not express total despair: the young do not have to be protected in this way. . . .

The prose has a very positive sound to it; an appealing music in its cadences; an appropriateness in its images:

> So they drove and his father recited some fragments of Thomas Wolfe, about October and the tumbling leaves of bitter red, or yellow leaves like living light, and Adam was sad again, thinking of his father as a writer and how his life had changed, how it had become necessary for him to give up all that and become another person altogether, how all of them had become other persons, his father, his mother, and himself. Paul Delmonte, poor lost Paul Delmonte.

In such a passage as this is the kind of compromise that is not obvious, because it lies beneath the surface of the narrative: Adam sadly accepting the fugitive existence to which he and his parents have been reduced is inevitable.

Excerpted from David Rees, *The Marble in the Water: Essays on Contemporary Writers of Fiction for Children and Young Adults.* The Horn Book, Inc., 1980. Copyright © 1980 by David Rees. Reprinted by permission of The Horn Book, Inc., 56 Roland St., Suite 200, Boston, MA 02129, 617-628-0225

Chronology

1925
Robert Edmund Cormier was born in Leominster, Massachusetts, on January 17.

1929
The stock market crashes on October 24 and marks the onset of the Great Depression.

1939
The apartment house where Cormier's family lives burns to the ground. Cormier graduates from St. Cecilia's parochial school.

1941
On December 7, the Japanese attack Pearl Harbor. Four days later, the United States enters World War II.

1942
Cormier graduates from Leominster High School.

1943
After being rejected by the Army, Cormier enrolls at Fitchburg State Teacher's College.

1944
In May: Cormier publishes "The Little Things That Count" in *The Sign* magazine.

1945
World War II ends and the Cold War between the United States and the U.S.S.R. begins.

1946
Takes a job with WTAG writing commercials.

1948
On November 6, marries Constance Senay. Takes a position as a reporter for the Worcester *Telegram & Gazette*.

1950
The United States enters the Korean War.

1951
Daughter Roberta is born.

1953
Son Peter is born

1955
Takes a job as a reporter with the *Fitchburg Sentinel*.

1957
Daughter Christine is born.

1959
Promoted to wire editor at the *Fitchburg Sentinel*. Awarded best human interest story of the year by the Associated Press in New England.

1960
Publishes first novel, *Now and At the Hour*.

1962
U.S. helicopters and troops begin to take a limited role in the fighting in Vietnam.

1963
A Little Raw on Monday Mornings is published. It is Cormier's second novel.

1964
Begins writing a book review column, "The Sentinel Bookman," for the *Fitchburg Sentinel*.

1965
Third novel, *Take Me Where the Good Times Are*, is published.

1966
Promoted to associate editor of the *Fitchburg Sentinel*.

1967
Daughter Renee is born.

1969
Begins a second column for the *Sentinel*. It is a human interest column that he writes under the pseudonym John Fitch IV.

1972
Begins writing a monthly human interest column, "1177 Main Street," for the *St. Anthony Messenger*.

1973
Again awarded best human interest story of the year by the Associated Press of New England.

1974
The Chocolate War is published. It is voted "Outstanding Book of the Year" by the *New York Times* and "Best Book for Young Adults" by the American Library Association. Cormier also receives best newspaper column award by K. R. Thomson Newspapers, Inc.

1976
Awarded Maxi Award by *Media and Methods* for *The Chocolate War.*

1977
I Am the Cheese is published. Like its predecessor, this novel is also voted "Outstanding Book of the Year" by the *New York Times* and "Best Book for Young Adults" by the American Library Association. Receives honorary Doctor of Letters from Fitchburg State College.

1978
Leaves *Fitchburg Sentinel* to write full time. Awarded Woodward School Annual Book Award for *I Am the Cheese.*

1979
After the First Death published. This is also voted "Outstanding Book of the Year" by the *New York Times* and "Best Book for Young Adults" by the American Library Association. Cormier is further awarded the Lewis Carroll Shelf Award for *The Chocolate War.*

1980
Eight Plus One is published. It receives "Notable Children's Trade Book in the Field of Social Studies" citation from the National Council for Social Studies and Children's Book Council.

1981
Robert E. Cormier Collection established at Fitchburg State College.

1982
Receives Assembly on Literature for Adolescents (ALAN) Award from the National Council of Teachers of English.

1983
The motion picture *I Am the Cheese* is released. *The Bumblebee Flies Away* is published. It is voted "Best Book for Young Adults" by the

American Library Association and "Best Book of 1983" by *School Library Journal*. Cormier also receives "Best of the Best Books, 1970–1983" citations from the American Library Association for *The Chocolate War, I Am the Cheese,* and *After the First Death.* Furthermore, he is presented with the Reader's Choice Award for the short story "President Cleveland Where Are You?" in *Eight Plus One.*

1985
Beyond the Chocolate War is published.

1986
Awarded Horn Book "Honor List" citation for *Beyond the Chocolate War.*

1988
Fade is published. It is awarded Young Adult Services Division Best Book for Young Adults citation by the American Library Association.

1989
Fall of the Berlin Wall marks the end of the Cold War; receives World Fantasy Award nomination for *Fade*. The Motion picture *The Chocolate War* is released.

1990
Other Bells Ring for Us, illustrated by Deborah Kogan, is published.

1991
We All Fall Down and *I Have Words to Spend* are published. Receives Margaret A. Edwards Award from the American Library Association for *The Chocolate War, I Am the Cheese,* and *After the First Death.*

1992
Tunes for Bears to Dance To is published.

1995
In the Middle of the Night is published.

1997
Tenderness is published.

1998
Heroes: A Novel is published.

1999
Frenchtown Summer is published.

Works Consulted

Major Editions of *I Am the Cheese*

Robert Cormier, *I Am the Cheese*. New York: Pantheon, 1977.
Robert Cormier, *I Am the Cheese*. London: Victor Gollancz, 1977.
Robert Cormier, *I Am the Cheese*. New York: Dell Laurel-Leaf, 1978.
[third reprint (1991) is used for quotes in this book]
Robert Cormier, *I Am the Cheese*. NY: Pantheon, 1997. Twentieth anniversary hardcover reissue of novel.
Robert Cormier, *I Am the Cheese*. Topeka, KS: Econo-Clad Books, 1999. Contains new introduction by Cormier.

Also by Robert Cormier

Robert Cormier, *The Chocolate War*. New York: Dell Laurel-Leaf, 1974. Cormier's first young adult novel, it tells the story of Jerry Renault's struggle against his private school society.

———,"The Cormier Novels: The Cheerful Side of Controversy," *Catholic Library World*, July/August 1978. Cormier tells the story of a protest of *The Chocolate War*, discusses his approach to writing for young adults, and discloses some of his writing secrets.

———, *Eight Plus One: Stories by Robert Cormier*. New York: Pantheon Books, 1980. A collection of stories that Cormier wrote from 1965–1975, it also contains an introduction by the author.

———, *I Have Words to Spend: Reflections of a Small-Town Editor*. New York: Delacorte Press, 1991. This is a collection of some of the pieces that Cormier wrote for his "And So On" column with the *Fitchburg Sentinel*. The book was edited and contains an introduction written by Constance Senay Cormier, his wife.

———, "Forever Pedaling on the Road to Realism,"in Betsy Hearne and Marilyn Kaye, ed., *Celebrating Children's Books: Essays on Children's Literature in Honor of Zena Sutherland*. New York: Lothrup, Lee & Shepard Books, 1981. Cormier discusses the realistic nature of his young adult fiction.

Biographical Information

Patricia J. Campbell, *Presenting Robert Cormier*. Boston: Twayne Publishers, 1985. The first few chapters of this book represent the most thorough biography of Robert Cormier to 1985. Campbell combined biographical information with an extensive interview of Cormier. The book also discusses Cormier's work up until 1985.

Robert Cormier, e-mail to author, November 12, 1999. In this e-mail, Cormier responded to a variety of questions asked by the author of this work.

Contemporary Authors: New Revision Series, s.v. "Cormier, Robert." Volume 23 contains a short biography of Cormier as well as a very useful interview.

Geraldine DeLuca and Roni Natov, "An Interview with Robert Cormier," *The Lion and the Unicorn: A Critical Journal of Children's Literature,* Spring 1978. An excellent, twenty-plus page interview with Robert Cormier conducted one year after the publication of *I Am the Cheese.*

Dictionary of Literary Biography: Volume 52 American Writers for Children Since 1960: Fiction. Detroit, MI: Gale Research Company, 1986. Part of a biographical reference series about authors, this volume contains information on Robert Cormier.

Laurel Graeber, "PW Interviews: Robert Cormier," *Publishers Weekly,* October 7, 1983. A short interview with Cormier right before the publication of *Bumblebee Flies Away.*

Paul Janeczko, "In Their Own Words: An Interview with Robert Cormier," *English Journal,* September 1977. A short interview with Robert Cormier conducted a few months after *I Am the Cheese* was released.

Robert C. Laserte, "History and Description of Leominster, Massachusetts," http://ci.leominster.ma.us/aboutleo.htm. This is part of the City of Leominster's website. On this page, former president of the Leominster Historical Society, Robert Laserte, describes the city and tells a bit about its history.

Merri Rosenberg, "Teen-Agers Face Evil," *New York Times Book Review,* May 5, 1985. An interview with Robert Cormier that focuses on his view of the teenage audience for whom he writes.

Tony Schwartz, "Teen-Agers' Laureate," *Newsweek,* July 16, 1979. A short piece on Cormier that provides some useful biographical information.

Anita Silvey, "An Interview with Robert Cormier," *Horn Book Magazine,* March/April 1985. Another useful interview.

Something About the Author, "Cormier, Robert." Several volumes of this series contain articles about Cormier. In particular, vol. 45 contains portions of a useful 1982 interview.

Roger Sutton, "A Conversation with Robert Cormier: 'Kind of a Funny Dichotomy,'" *School Library Journal,* June 1991. In a very good interview with Cormier, Sutton asks a variety of questions that were not touched upon in previous interviews.

Young Adult Fiction Historical Background

Joan Glazer and Gurnery Williams III, *Introduction to Children's Literature*. New York: McGraw-Hill, 1979. Contains some information on the historical evolution of young adult fiction, realism, the problem novel, and New Realism.

Donna E. Norton, *Through the Eyes of a Child: An Introduction to Children's Literature*. New York: MacMillan Publishing Company, Merrill, 1991. The second chapter of this book provides a history of young adult fiction that is quite useful in understanding the development of the category over time.

Literary Reviews and Criticism

M. H. Abrams, *A Glossary of Literary Terms*. Fort Worth, TX: Harcourt Brace Jovanovich College Publishers, 1993. Provides a useful definition of realism.

Robert Bell, *"I Am the Cheese," The School Librarian*, September 1978. A short review of the novel.

Phyllis Bixler, *"I Am the Cheese* and Reader-Response Criticism in the Adolescent Literature Classroom," *Children's Literature in Education*, Spring 1985. Bixler discusses the results of a reader-response assignment she assigned her class.

Booklist, "Books for Young Adults," April 1, 1977. Contains an early review of *I Am the Cheese*.

Newgate Callendar, "Boy on the Couch," *The New York Times Book Review*, May 1, 1977. An early review of *I Am the Cheese*.

J. A. Cuddon, *A Dictionary of Literary Terms*. Cambridge, MA: Basil Blackwell Inc., 1991. Provides a useful definition and discussion of literary realism.

Kenneth L. Donelson and Alleen Pace Nilsen, *Literature for Today's Young Adults*. New York: Harper Collins Publishers, 1989. Contains a very useful chapter on New Realism as well as a discussion of *I Am the Cheese* as an example of traditional literary tragedy.

Margery Fisher, "Significant Forms," *Growing Point*, April 1978. A brief review and discussion of technique in *I Am the Cheese*.

Patricia Head, "Robert Cormier and the Postmodernist Possibilities of Young Adult Fiction," *Children's Literature Association Quarterly*, Spring 1996. Discusses the ways in which Cormier's work is postmodern and the avenues it opens up in young adult fiction.

Paul Heins, "*I Am the Cheese,*" *Horn Book Magazine,* August 1977. A short review of the novel.

Sylvia Patterson Iskander, "Readers, Realism, and Robert Cormier," *Children's Literature: Annual of the Modern Language Association Division on Children's Literature and the Children's Literature Association,* 1987. Iskander uses Jonathan Culler's work with verisimilitude to argue that Cormier intentionally goes against readers' expectations in order to force them to action and political responsibility.

The Junior Bookshelf, June 1978. A review of *I Am the Cheese.*

Joyce Kinkead and Patricia Stoddart, "YA Books in the Classroom: Pen-Pals and *I Am the Cheese,*" *The ALAN Review,* Fall 1987. These two educators discuss the pen-pal method that they used to bring their college and high school classes (respectively) together in reading *I Am the Cheese.*

Audrey Laski, "No Laughing Matter: Audrey Laski on Fiction for Young Adults," *The Times Educational Supplement,* November 18, 1977. In this review of *I Am the Cheese* Laski expresses displeasure with the direction that young adult fiction is going.

Richard R. Lingeman, "Boy in a Trap," *The New York Times Book Review,* May 22, 1977. A review of *I Am the Cheese* comparing Cormier's work to that of spy novelist John le Carré.

C. M. (sic), "Catchers in the Rye," *Newsweek,* December 19, 1977. A hearty recommendation of *I Am the Cheese* for parents.

Anne Scott MacLeod, "Robert Cormier and the Adolescent Novel," *Children's Literature in Education,* Summer 1981. MacLeod argues that Cormier's novels send a positive political message to his readers.

Robbie March-Penny, "From Hardback to Paperback: *The Chocolate War,* by Robert Cormier," *Children's Literature in Education,* Summer 1978. Contains a brief discussion of the plight of the individual versus the system in *I Am the Cheese.*

Maia Pank Mertz, "Enhancing Literary Understandings Through Young Adult Fiction," *Publishing Research Quarterly,* Spring 1992. Contains a brief discussion of the structure and style of *I Am the Cheese.*

Joseph Milner, ed., *Webs and Wardrobes: Humanist and Religious World Views in Children's Literature.* Lanham, MD: University Press of America, 1987. Contains an essay by Rebecca Lukens, who argues that in the thirty years between Salinger's *The Catcher in the Rye* and Cormier's work the world view of popular literature flipped from disillusionment to despair.

Perry Nodelman, "Robert Cormier Does a Number," *Children's Literature in Education*, Summer 1983. Nodelman provides an in-depth discussion of the structure of *I Am the Cheese*.

William J. O'Malley, "A Review of *I Am the Cheese*," *Media & Methods*, May/June 1978. A review of *I Am the Cheese*.

Alleen Pace Nilsen, "The Poetry of Naming in Young Adult Books," *The ALAN Review*, Spring 1980. A discussion of the significance of the names chosen for characters in various Cormier novels.

Publishers Weekly, March 7, 1977. An early review of *I Am the Cheese*.

David Rees, *The Marble in the Water: Essays on Contemporary Writers of Fiction for Children and Young Adults*. Boston: The Horn Book Company, Inc., 1980. Rees's book contains an essay on Cormier and Jill Chaney.

Lance Salway, "Death and Destruction," *Times Literary Supplement*, December 2, 1977. A review of *I Am the Cheese* that briefly discusses the usefulness of the novel's structure.

Roger Sutton, "The Critical Myth: Realistic YA Novels," *School Library Journal*, November 1982. Sutton argues that New Realism is not the "hard-hitting" and "shattering" realism critics have talked it up to be. Instead, he believes that young adult fiction does not really challenge readers. Sutton deals with Cormier as one example of New Realism.

Nancy Veglahn, "The Bland Face of Evil in the Novels of Robert Cormier," *The Lion and the Unicorn: A Critical Journal of Children's Literature*, June 1988. An excellent discussion about the representation of evil in Cormier's novels.

Index

Picture Credits

About the Author

Jennifer Keeley is a freelance writer who lives and works in Seattle, Washington. She graduated from Carleton College in 1996 with a degree in history and her teaching certificate. She has taught history and social studies in both the Seattle and Minneapolis Public Schools.